BRIDGE ACROSS TROUBLED WATERS

BRIDGE ACROSS TROUBLED WATERS

Centering Prayer and the Theological Divide

≈

KESS FREY

FOREWORD BY FR. THOMAS KEATING

LINDISFARNE BOOKS | 2017

2017
Lindisfarne Books
An imprint of Anthroposophic Press / SteinerBooks
610 Main St., Great Barrington, MA
www.steinerbooks.org

Design by Jens Jensen
Cover image Suspension Bridge © by Sergii Votit

≈

LIBRARY OF CONGRESS CONTROL NUMBER: 2017936806

ISBN: 978-1-58420-956-0 (paperback)
ISBN: 978-1-58420-957-7 (eBook)

CONTENTS

This book is dedicated to T. K. and to all who study, practice, and teach the Christian Contemplative Tradition.

ACKNOWLEDGMENTS

In addition to invisible sources of inspiration and guidance, I am deeply grateful and indebted to the wisdom, teaching, and support of Thomas Keating. It was Fr. Carl Arico asking me, in November 2015, to answer some criticism of Centering Prayer and Thomas Keating's teaching that led eventually to writing this book. Encouragement, suggestions, and feedback from Carl J. Arico and Maru Ladron de Guevara have been very helpful, and especially Maru's suggestion and contributions to section titles in the book's chapters. I thank George Provost for his input early on; Donna Davis for information about T. M.; and Pamela Begeman for suggesting "The Church in the Wilderness" paper as a resource. I am also grateful to Jens Jensen for his good work on the book design and cover image.

AUTHOR'S NOTE

My best writing is a gift transmitted to and through me from a higher spiritual Source. When I read it myself, I go only so far as I enjoy and feel fully engaged with the text, taking time to reflect on the words and to digest each section before going on to the next. Most of my writing is like this; that is, deeply condensed, needs to be gradually digested, and not intended for "speed reading." If reading becomes difficult or tedious, I realize I have read my fill for now, stop and go back or give it a rest. As with a meal, it's best to eat only a limited amount at each sitting, returning to the table when you feel hungry again—read a little later or maybe the next day when your mind is fresh.

In this way, we may get much more out of spiritual books and sacred texts—being patient, taking our time, and not trying to take in too much all at once. A contemplative approach of abiding peacefully in the present moment and reading a bit at a time allows one to reflect on the text and to consciously digest its deeper meaning and more subtle nuances. Ideally, and to fully enter into the spirit of this or any of my books, *Bridge across Troubled Waters* may be read aloud, slowly, and thoughtfully, in a whispered voice as a private meditation. Such conscious engagement with the book does, I believe, greatly facilitate the intuitive transmission of the text's living nonverbal essence to the receptive reader.

K. F.

FOREWORD

THOMAS KEATING

This book is a major contribution to Contemplative Outreach literature. For the first time, a careful and comprehensive response to criticisms leveled against Centering Prayer is presented. Kess Frey, with his long-time practice of the prayer, previous books, retreats, and workshops, is in an ideal position to speak to the problems with Centering Prayer that some people have expressed in articles, books, and on TV. He believes the basic problem lies in the theological understanding, or rather misunderstanding, of the Christian contemplative tradition.

According to Frey, seekers of God are looking at the same phenomenon from two radically different theological points of view. What they see and how they react depend on deeply held belief systems that evaluate faith teachings and spiritual experiences from two different perspectives. One of these belief systems is called "the Western Model" of self-outside-God and God-outside-the-self. The other is called "the Scriptural Model" of the-self-in-God and God-in-the self. "Western" refers to the theology taught for the last few centuries that emphasizes God's transcendence with little or inadequate reference to God's all embracing immanence in all of creation, especially in human beings.

The Scriptural Model draws its inspiration from the Gospel which Jesus refers to as "the Good News." It is based in a special way on the teaching of Jesus at the Last Supper regarding his abiding indwelling within us, together with the Father and the Holy Spirit.

This distinction between the Western Model and the Scriptural Model was first described in the book, *In His Spirit*, by Father Richard Hauser, S.J. (Paulist Press, 1982). Frey explains both models in great detail and further develops the insightful teaching of Fr. Hauser in terms of Centering Prayer's conceptual background.

The Good News that Jesus reveals in the Gospel is that God loves us, is present within us always, and seeks to transform us into his own divine light, life, and love. This teaching needs to come first in religious instruction. Without the conviction of God's boundless mercy and love for us, we are not likely to make the effort to love others, especially our enemies.

In the Western model, we are represented as initiating all our good works and God rewards. In the Scriptural Model, the Holy Spirit inspires all our good works and we consent. This teaching enables an ever deeper relationship with Jesus and growth into increasing intimacy with God. It also can open the way for Christians to live in a deeper communion of respect and love for each other and to grow in compassion for all humanity.

Frey urges us to build bridges between the Scriptural and Western Models, and together build up the Body of Christ. *Bridge across Troubled Waters* describes how, in the Scriptural Model and our deepening relationship with God, the Western Model is gradually transcended and integrated so that the values of both are preserved and enhanced.

PREFACE

This book is written in response to a variety of misconceptions and criticisms in regard to Centering Prayer. It is written to explore the intimacy of the divine relationship we all have with God since our soul's creation. Criticisms of Centering Prayer range from the overly cautious to the suspiciously fearful and the patently absurd—even equating this prayer to "playing with an Ouija Board" and contacting "evil spirits." Leaving aside absurd extremes, *Bridge across Troubled Waters* seeks to build a healing bridge of communication across the divide of troubled waters separating sincere Christians who embrace Centering Prayer from those who may fear or oppose it. Misunderstanding and misinformation regarding Centering Prayer and its conceptual background seem to be the primary source of its criticisms and misinterpretations.

This book seeks Christian unity and addresses questions such as: Is Centering Prayer Christian? Is it dangerous? Does it conflict with the teaching of the Catholic Church? For whom is Centering Prayer appropriate? In answering these questions and others, the book explores our divine relationship with God in the context of Centering Prayer's conceptual background and the living history of our Christian Contemplative Heritage—which many contemporary Christians have heard little or nothing about. There's room for all ways of praying (relating to God) under the "Big Tent" of the Christian Faith; and each person has a need and right to pray in the ways that they feel are right for them. All sincere Christian prayer is in the service of our spiritual growth in the divine relationship into which our loving God invites us. Our deepening relationship with God ripens and matures through the gift of silent contemplation—for which Centering Prayer prepares us.

Bridge across Troubled Waters is intended for individuals who are curious about Centering Prayer and who may have been exposed to some of its criticisms, so that they may learn about it from the perspective of one who advocates Centering Prayer and then make up their own mind. This book is intended for doubters and critics of the prayer, as an invitation to peacefully view it from another perspective, and to invite reconsideration of this prayer in a spirit of Christian charity, tolerance, and reconciliation. *Bridge across Troubled Waters* is intended for anyone interested in these issues and in a new way of seeing the eternal two-way relationship we all have with our Divine Source and spiritual Father.

INTRODUCTION

Dear Brothers and Sisters in Christ,

Please read this detailed essay slowly and gradually. Its intent is to promote Christian unity and harmony among all people. For this to succeed, your openness of heart and mind, as well as your willingness to think in more than one way, are needed. We always have a choice to open or close our hearts and minds. Whenever we are willing to consider alternate views and their implications, we may then be free to consciously decide which view or combination of views best rings true and makes sense to us. Though universal spiritual principles, such as love, truth, and freedom do not change, our understanding and appreciation of the Spirit's eternal values do change. As we learn and grow, our views of love, truth, freedom, and other divine qualities will change and evolve correspondingly. Consciously considering new possibilities from outside the box of our preconceived ideas can be an exciting adventure of heart and mind for us all. God has so much more than we may possibly imagine of goodness and wonder, of love, truth, and freedom waiting in store for us! (cf. 1 Cor. 2:9).

As we explore divides in human consciousness, and the theological divide in particular, may negative attitudes of defensiveness and judgment be set aside. May they be replaced by goodwill and curiosity to discover in the other something new and true we didn't know before. Let us choose, at least for a time, to assume those with different views are well meaning, sincere, and acting in good faith from within the knowledge of their own perspectives. In this way, we may seek reconciliation and understanding. So let us choose not to mistrust, demonize, or assume those with different views are knowingly or unknowingly agents of ignorance, ill will, or evil. What would Jesus ask us to do in our openness to and relations with one another?

In John's Gospel, Jesus gives us his new commandment: "Love one another as I have loved you" (John 15:12). He also tells us: "By your love for one another they will know you are my disciples" (John 13:35). Now what does this love do? It reaches out, overflowing the heart's boundaries and all boundaries of separation; and it co-identifies with others in the deeper sense of Christ's presence within us all. This is a radical holy love. Christian love seeks mutual reconciliation, understanding, and forgiveness wherever these are needed; knowing that whatever we do or don't do to one another, we do or don't do to Christ in one another. Hence, how we treat others around us directly affects our relationship to Christ within us. Jesus makes this clear in Matthew 25:31–45 where he says that whatever is done to even the least of human beings is done unto him.

This statement is grounded in the central Christian insight that Christ dwells deeply in all of us. The conviction of Christ's living presence in all people is foundational to a fully awakened Catholic Christian faith and its practical applications in our daily lives and relationships. It's based on what Holy Scripture, the written Word of God, actually tells us (see, for example, John 1:1–4). Unfortunately, though understandably (as we shall see), some Christians may doubt the truth of Christ's dwelling in all people; and this becomes the basis of some unfortunate misunderstandings and a needless theological divide among sincere Christians.

Love for others is the hallmark of a true Christian. This love for one another is not meant just for fellow Christians, for those who agree with us, or who are sincerely seeking to practice the Gospel of Jesus. Love for one another is meant to be practiced in relation to everyone, including our enemies. This is Jesus' radical teaching that challenges us to outgrow the limitations and prejudices of our separate-self-identity and cultural conditioning. Jesus makes this clear in Matthew 5:44, where—going against the common-sense practicality of our typical human-ground thinking—he says, "But I say to you, love your enemies, and pray for those who persecute you."

With this in mind, it seems incumbent on us as Christians to seek peace, harmony, reconciliation, and unity with our beloved fellow Christians and with all humanity, to whatever extent this is possible. Clearly, some degree of mutual cooperation, trust, and willingness to really listen and hear one another are needed to make this aim a reality. Wherever such mutuality is lacking, we may only love one another across whatever divides separate us—such as theological divides between the outer and the inner, between the rational and the mystical, between duality (separation) and non-duality (union). The wedge of these divides is driven by our mutual failures to truly hear, trust, and understand one another in humility and empathy as human beings and spiritual beings in the Body of Christ.

Our Common Ground, Human and Spiritual

Our Soul's Inner Wealth

We are both human beings rooted in human ground and spiritual beings rooted in spiritual ground, all of us. This is the universal basis of humanity's common ground. As human beings, we share a common human nature and needs that are universal throughout the human family. At the same time, we are all distinct individuals with particular social, cultural, family, sexual, racial, ethnic, national, political, economic, educational, historical, and religious backgrounds that serve as the basis of our unique identities in human ground. Hence, we are all both the same and different as human beings. While our sameness unites us, our differences often divide us.

As spiritual beings, we all come from the same divine Source—which we may call by various names in various human languages. For Christians and others, the name "God" is commonly used to refer to the divine Source of our being. There are, of course, many humanly created and divinely inspired ideas of God in the world—none of which can be perfect, absolute, or complete, and all of which are human attempts to grasp and relate to the inconceivable Mystery of God Who transcends and includes created reality and everything in it. The Divine—however we conceive it—is our sacred Source of ultimate meaning and value in life.

Theology is concerned with human ideas about God or Ultimate Reality, and it's concerned with our eternal relationship to God. Since all our ideas of God are limited and exist within created reality, none of them may possibly give us the fullness of God's Divine Reality—which is limitless and beyond created reality. Our limited ideas of

God may, however, be helpful to us as stepping stones for relating to God—Who knows each of us intimately through and through, and is inviting us into the divine relationship (which already exists from God's side of the relationship since our creation as individual souls).

The theological ideas inherent to the above statements regarding God and the divine relationship are based, in part, on my interpretation of the first three chapters of the Book of Genesis. This perspective and more is expressed in detail in my book, *Human Ground Spiritual Ground, Paradise Lost and Found: A Reflection on Centering Prayer's Conceptual Background.* What we are calling "the theological divide" arises only in human ground, when individuals with differing, competing ideas of God and our relationship to God disagree and see each other as wrong or in error. There is no theological divide in spiritual ground, where truth is immediately revealed. It's only on the human level where there may be real or imagined divides between our outer human ground and the inner spiritual ground that unites us.

The theological divide may take various forms and is typical of all divides that take expression in human consciousness and relationships. Most common among these is the divide between our outer human life and our inner spiritual life. If we're to grow as human beings and spiritual beings, at some point we each must come to realize that the outer world is not all that there is. There is an inner spiritual world and life that we are all rooted in, and this inner reality of our being endures beyond the temporary drama and game of our outer life and human identity. If we fail to realize this—that is, if we fail to realize that we are spiritual beings with an inner spiritual life and relationship to God, as well as human beings living in the world—then we miss the real treasure of our inner depths and remain stuck on life's surface where changing conditions and appearances rise and fall like waves on the ocean that crest and crash without root or depth in the ground of their Source.

The word *religion* in the English language comes from the Latin *religare*—which means "to bind back to origins." Hence, the true and original purpose or role of religion is to put us into living contact and harmonious relationship with the divine Source or Ground of our being, i.e., God. In doing so, religion's proper function is to guide us into authentic meaning, value, fulfillment, and relationship in our human and spiritual lives. Our soul's inner wealth comes to us in human ground and spiritual ground through the loving generosity, outreach, mercy, and compassion of our divine Source. As individual souls created in the divine image and likeness (Gen. 1:26–27), we each have a divine inheritance from God that is held in store for us within us. Religion's chief or highest function in the service of God's Will is to give us practical access to this divine inheritance.

God's loving Will and intention are for us to come into full possession of our divine inheritance as God's spiritual children; but this may happen only on God's terms, not ours. As Paul writes in Romans 8:16–17: "The Spirit itself bears witness with our spirit that we are children of God, and if children, then heirs, heirs of God and joint heirs with Christ, if only we suffer with him so that we may also be glorified with him." The suffering of which Paul writes here involves the inner death of our sinful worldly nature (*the flesh,* or false self of our human personality), so that we may be reborn in Christ (*the Spirit,* or true self of our divine inheritance). What this spiritual rebirth actually is remains to be discovered.

WHAT DOES LOVE WANT?

In his book, *Invitation to Love,* Thomas Keating points out that we are all born with certain basic instinctual needs that must be met to some minimal degree if we're to survive and thrive in this life. Following from Thomas Keating's work, I identify these basic needs as follows: security/survival/safety; sensation/pleasure; affection/esteem/approval; power/control; and intimacy/belonging. Our basic instinctual needs are all interrelated and take expression on every level of our being: that is, the physical, vital, emotional, mental, psychic, social, and spiritual levels. Our true needs give rise to inborn desires about which we have no choice. We are all hardwired or preprogrammed with our basic instinctual needs. We do, however, have choices regarding how we go about trying to meet these needs.

Our survival instinct, which we share with all other life forms, is the most basic of our needs. In human beings, the survival instinct is a psychospiritual need as well as a physical one. It's our need for security, survival, and safety on all levels of our being—which include our physical, vital, emotional, mental, psychic, social, and spiritual levels. From this perspective, we may see that religious beliefs, theology, and our inner spiritual life play central roles in meeting our need for security/survival/safety on the deepest ontological level (the level of being), which goes beyond our temporary life and ego identity as a human being. This is important to bear in mind when thinking about the opposite sides of a theological divide, as it may help us to empathically understand the psychological basis of another's feelings of emotional attachment to particular ideas regarding God and our relationship to God. That is, we need to honor the fact that the specifics of religious faith are often a source of another's ontological security.

The universal human need for security/survival/safety is a legitimate need and right for every human being; and it's an important basis of humanity's common ground. In relating to others, it's wise to compassionately consider how what we say or do may impact their inner psychospiritual security/survival center. Most of us need to feel that there's a positive future for our survival in both this world and/or the next. People are liable to become uneasy or defensive if what we say threatens their sense of security on any level. Guiding and reassuring us in the area of ontological security in this life and beyond is a primary function of religious teaching, practice, and experience.

For most of us, our personal belief system and theological perspective have a direct bearing on the psychospiritual aspect of our basic need for security/survival/safety. This is often an emotionally charged issue that we need to respect when relating to fellow Christians or others with different views and theologies. People sometimes become overly attached to their beliefs because they depend on them to feel safe and secure in the face of existential uncertainty. In contrast to this, other individuals may try to avoid this core issue—the issue of our mortality—by ignoring it; but ultimately the "ostrich technique" of denial and hiding our head in the sand will not work. In any case, we all know on some level of our being that human life is a temporary affair. A key existential question is: What comes next? This question goes to the heart of our deep common need for security/survival/safety on the ontological level.

Another complementary key question is: What does God want? How we answer these two key questions depends on what we believe, what we assume to be true, and/or what we feel in our heart. As to what happens next (following our physical death): either something or nothing will happen. If it's nothing, as atheistic materialists believe, then our physical death is the end of our story. If something does happen after death, then there are many possibilities to imagine. Which of these possibilities we embrace or choose will depend on our theological perspective or idea of God—Who is running the show of created reality. Faith-filled trust in God's goodness allows us to feel secure and to tolerate uncertainty without needing to know the complete answer to "What happens next?" This naturally brings up the second key question: "What does God want?" How we answer this key question may place us on one or the other side of a theological divide. In all of this, we may see some examples of how we're united in our common need for security/survival/safety; and also how we may become divided by clinging to particular dogmatic answers to these key questions to the exclusion of other answers. Understanding these differences, honoring everyone's need for security/survival/safety, and allowing room for differing viewpoints all have much to do with reconciling theological differences.

If, following what's written in 1 John 4:8, 16, we accept the idea that "God is love," and the tremendous implications of this idea, then we may rephrase the second key question to ask: "What does Love want?"[1] This is indeed a deep question to ponder. It holds within it the truest answers to both of the above key questions. Love and death are the great equalizers in created reality that return us all to our common ground and origins in God. If we really trust in the goodness of God's love, then we shall have no difficulty with "What happens next?" and "What does God want?" Lacking such faith in God or Nature, we're liable to experience fear, anxiety, doubt, and to find ourselves in need of guarantees and reassurances from religious or other authorities. Or else we may try the "ostrich technique" of avoiding the issue.

Our Common Ground and Deep Healing

As mentioned above, every human being has a need for security/survival/safety: materially and spiritually, emotionally and mentally, socially and privately. By exploring the deep reach of this most basic need into our life, we may notice that our basic instinctual needs are all closely interconnected, acting and reacting upon one another. The meeting of each of our basic needs gives us a feeling of wellbeing and contributes to the fulfillment of our overall need for security/survival/safety. For example, the healthy meeting of our need for sensation/pleasure is life-affirming and gives us a positive attitude about human existence and the goodness of what life has to offer. Various forms of sensation/pleasure are experienced in the meeting of all our needs or desires. This may make us glad and grateful to be alive—which in turn affirms and reinforces our security/survival need, motivating us to want more of life.

Our need for affection/esteem/approval is essentially an emotional one. Without emotional security, we may experience little happiness or peace of mind. In early life and later, on the social level of human relationships, we depend on others to help us meet this basic need. We may see this in the amount of importance people pay to what others think, feel, and say about them on the social and interpersonal levels. It's also seen in the lengths to which we and others may go to create "a good impression" and to get others to like, admire, or accept us. A lot of time, energy, and money are spent in pursuing emotional security via impressing or pleasing others in various ways to meet our emotional need for affection/esteem/approval.

As we grow up and mature emotionally, we become less dependent on others for emotional security and for meeting our need for affection/esteem/approval. This happens as we grow in healthy self-esteem and gain the freedom and independence of becoming our own person through deepening self-knowledge and living in harmony with our innate spiritual conscience. The individual freedom and independence this gives us help us to meet our healthy need for power/control as well. In early life, we're dependent on the care and respect of others to meet our needs for security/survival/safety and affection/esteem/approval. We possess very little power/control in early life. As we grow up emotionally and mature into healthy human beings, we tend to become more emotionally self-reliant and less dependent on others to meet our needs. The greatest fulfillment of our need for affection/esteem/approval comes when we feel inwardly affirmed in our relationship with God.

Emotional self-reliance happens as we grow a healthy sense of self-esteem by being true to our self and living in harmony with our conscience. We develop a center of moral/ethical integrity within us that supports our sense of self-worth and that's affirmed by our conscience—which is the inner voice of divine wisdom and guidance God has placed in our soul. Our true conscience is the inner Advocate for our spiritual growth and relationship with God, once we can hear and follow it. Jesus refers to our spiritual conscience in John 14:16–17, 26 as *"another Advocate to be with you always, the Spirit of Truth— he will teach you everything and remind you of all that I told you."* True conscience is the inner rock or foundation for the development of healthy self-esteem. Living in harmony with conscience naturally gives us self-respect, inner peace, and clarity of thought. These are qualities of good mental health that we all need to feel whole in our self and in right relationship with God.

Inner peace and clarity of thought form a foundation for the healthy expression of our basic need for power/control. Power/control is essentially a mental need based on our skills, gifts, understanding, and accurate information regarding what is going on inside us, with others, and in the world around us. Knowledge is power. Ignorance is weakness or blindness. Our healthy need for power/control is the need for personal independence and freedom in life. The legitimate meeting of this need allows us to meet all our basic needs, supports our security/survival/safety on the mental level, and reinforces our self-esteem on the emotional level. Healthy power/control grows out of our need for affection/esteem/approval. That is, if we feel secure and comfortable in our self on the emotional level, then we may develop the reassuring psychological security of healthy power/control on the mental level. When these are lacking, our human and spiritual growth get stunted and we may adopt rigid theological or other beliefs and attitudes for a semblance of certainty, and to compensate for what we inwardly fear is lacking in us. All of this relates to our security/survival/safety requisites on the emotional, mental, and spiritual levels.

Healthy power/control includes having a clear understanding of the situation in which we find ourselves, together with an orientation to life that integrates both the material and the spiritual dimensions of our existence. Knowing what is going on and discovering our purpose or where we fit into life are essential aspects of emotional security and healthy power/control. Such knowledge gives us a reassuring sense of existential stability and of belonging or place in life and the world.

Beyond affection/esteem/approval and power/control is our basic need for intimacy/belonging. This is both in relation to others and an inner spiritual need in relation to our self and God—the Divine Source of our being. Intimacy/belonging may be seen as a higher octave or expression of the need for affection/esteem/approval. Intimacy/belonging is essentially our soul's need for love. All experiences of authentic love, however brief or enduring, are actual experiences of God's presence (since, as Scripture tells us in 1 John 4:8, "*God is love*"). Love crosses all divides and creates instant connection, unity, co-identity, trust, and intimacy/belonging. Our sense of meaning in life comes from whatever we love, whatever we genuinely care about. If we care about nothing, then life becomes empty and meaningless for us. To have love in our life is to have God in our life. This is the heart's essence of intimacy/belonging that we all long for, whether we know it or not. Venturing into intimacy/belonging requires trust and always makes us vulnerable—whether it's to another person, God, our own unconscious, or whatever we commit to and place our trust in.

Expressing the soul's deepest spiritual necessity for intimacy/belonging (love) goes to the pinnacle of our hierarchy of needs. With whom or what we experience intimacy/belonging—which naturally leads to co-identification—depends on whom or what we care about. That is, it depends on where we invest the preciousness of our heart's treasure in human ground and/or spiritual ground. The measure of meaning we find in human life depends on the quality of whom or what we take seriously enough to truly love or care about. Love always brings something of God's presence into a relationship, whether we know it or not.

The greatest, most permanent fulfillment of our need for security/survival/safety is to be derived from growing intimacy/belonging in our inner spiritual relationship with God in spiritual ground. To truly and fully know our self is to know that we are rooted in God. Unlike our temporary life and relationships in changing human ground, our spiritual relationship with God is an eternal relationship. Hence, it's only the divine relationship that may offer us ultimate security/survival/safety. I feel it's safe to say that all Christians—whatever their theological perspectives may be—will agree with this statement.

DISTORTIONS AND EXAGGERATIONS

The facts that we, as humans, all have the same basic instinctual needs and that we're all created in God's image and likeness are important elements of our common ground. We are all both human beings and spiritual beings intimately connected and bound together in the love of Christ—Who is our ultimate common ground. Another important basis of our common ground is that we are all subject to the same inner wounding and afflictive emotions when our basic needs are neglected, abused, frustrated, or traumatized. This is especially acute in early life and continues throughout our time in this world. When our basic needs are not met, programs or drives to compensate for this are set up in the unconscious. Thomas Keating has called these "programs for happiness that can't possibly work."[2] These programs for happiness may be conscious or unconscious. In either case, they severely limit our personal freedom and may negatively influence us and our relationships throughout life, including our relationship with God, unless some deep healing takes place in our soul.

The symptoms of earlier-life and later-life wounding in our basic instinctual needs show up in adult life as distorted and exaggerated expressions of those needs that go far beyond the limits of their natural healthy expressions. For example, if a person's security/survival/safety need is damaged by trauma, abuse, or neglect in early or later life, he or she may feel compelled to compensate for this by seeking inordinate amounts of things that symbolize security/survival/safety in one's culture and belief system. These may include pursuing more and more material wealth and possessions in excess of what one legitimately or realistically needs. It may involve obsessions with physical security, health, and longevity via security alarm systems, insurance policies, and medical reassurances of one's wellbeing. Or, on the spiritual level, it may be expressed as an anxious need for guarantees of salvation and God's favor which are promised if one faithfully follows given requisite rules of thought, speech, feeling, and action.

Such emotional programs for happiness are easily rationalized and justified because they stem from what are legitimate requirements and concerns for virtually all of us, e.g., financial security, physical safety, and the soul's ontological wellbeing and survival. The problem with them is the extremity of their exaggerations and distortions beyond the levels of what we actually do need; how these emotional happiness programs keep us fixated in egocentric self-centeredness; and the extremes to which we may go to try to satisfy our unhealthy happiness programs. They become compulsive drives and obsessions motivated by inner attitudes of worry, doubt, fear, anger, and anxiety that no amount of gratification can keep satisfied as long as the unhealed wounds for which they are compensations persist in the unconscious. Hence, these unhealthy happiness programs enslave us and are aptly referred to by Thomas Keating as "programs for human misery."

Because of the emotional urgency we feel regarding them, our unhealthy happiness programs become top priorities for us that function as substitutes for God and serious obstacles to our spiritual growth and relationships with self, others, and the Divine. We all tend to see and interpret the world through the focusing lens of our personal issues, beliefs, and desires—and this includes the vision of our theological perspective. Our individual programs for happiness exert a powerful influence on how we perceive reality, other people, and how we relate to God. We tend to evaluate people, places, and things in terms of how they may serve the preconceived agendas of our self-centered happiness programs. This creates serious obstacles and limitations in our ability to be present in the now-moment and freely live the Gospel values of unselfish love, forgiveness, and service to others as taught by Jesus.

Some additional examples of unhealthy emotional happiness programs created unconsciously as compensations in response to the wounding of our basic instinctual needs are as follows: When our sensation/pleasure need is distorted and exaggerated, we may compulsively overindulge in things that provide us with various forms of sensation/pleasure. These may include entertainment, food abuse, alcohol, drugs, sex, gambling, sports, risky behavior, and pursuits of adventure/excitement, whatever gives us a laugh, a thrill, or the suspense of drama. Becoming a "pleasure junkie" is a path of diminishing returns that may provide fleeting experiences of pleasure, transcendence, or escape from one's unwanted normal reality; but ultimately it leads one into the humiliating slavery of unhealthy addictions and a hell of self-destructive behavior patterns.

Distortions and exaggerations of our basic need for affection/esteem/approval are often compensations for nagging self-doubt and painful emotional wounds from experiences of loss, loneliness, rejection, or abandonment. They may lead us into codependent relationships or compulsive "people-pleasing" behavior—where our own needs or desires are ignored or neglected for the sake of gaining affirmation or acceptance from another, others, or even God. There's a desperate drive for emotional security that takes top priority in our life and relationships when our affection/esteem/approval need is seriously wounded. Another way of trying to compensate for emotional neediness is by performing to impress others in all kinds of ways that may be public or private. The goal is to win admiration, affection, and respect from others, so that one may feel good about oneself. As with all happiness programs motivated by unhealed wounds in our basic needs, no matter how much we may get, it's never enough to keep us satisfied or give us lasting peace. These things have to come from within us; and until real healing takes place in the soul, our unhealed emotional wounds will keep haunting and nagging us from within the unconscious.

The frustration and wounding of our need for power/control gives rise to an unhealthy compensatory drive to exert power/control over situations and other people in various ways. This moves us to deprive others of their freedom and is the basis of considerable unnecessary conflict, war, and dishonesty in the human condition. Whether it's gross bullying or more subtle forms of intimidation, deception, trickery, and manipulation, all unhealthy power/control happiness programs create divides, isolation, loneliness, and resentment in human life and relationships. Aggressive warrior consciousness and the relentless drive for domination over others are unhealthy distortions and exaggerations of our wounded need for power/control. Equality, based on mutual trust and mutual respect, is the only reasonable basis for a healthy human relationship wherein love may grow. It's difficult for souls who've been wounded in their power/control need to really trust others and allow themselves to become vulnerable in a close, intimate relationship; this carries over into our relationship with God.

GROWING INTIMACY/BELONGING IN CLOSE PERSONAL RELATIONSHIPS

Intimacy/belonging is both a social need and a spiritual need involving our most important and dearest relationships with others, our groups, our self, and God. Intimacy/belonging pertains to what feels closest to us; that is, it pertains to our identity and allegiances as human beings and spiritual beings. To meet our important needs and desires, we tend to identify with whomever or whatever we feel close to, love, and look to. This includes our church, home, culture, friends, and society. We may or may not be conscious of our needs or how we try to meet them.

In early life and beyond, we naturally look outside our self to meet our basic cravings, including our need for love—for intimacy/belonging. We identify with our human parents and family of origin, and with all the groups to which we belong. Belonging gives us a secure sense of place in human life and the world, so we don't feel lost, isolated, and alone. In group-intimacy/belonging, we feel we are part of something greater than our separate-self; and we feel related to others who belong to the groups with which we identify. The things we share in common with members of our groups bond us to them and set us apart from the members of other groups that are different. We find a sense of tribal human identity in our social, cultural, religious, racial, ethnic, linguistic, national, sexual, economic, and other groups.

Intimacy creates a sense of belonging, and belonging creates a sense of intimacy. This intimacy/belonging is expressed on the group-identification level by our conformity to and acceptance of the characteristic styles, values, belief system, and worldview of our primary group(s). It's by means of such acceptance and conformity that we make a group our own and come to share its particular characteristics and qualities in common with other members of the group. Surface-to-deep feelings of mutual intimacy/belonging are thus created among the members of a particular group or community.

As we become increasingly identified with a group, we become likewise increasingly invested emotionally in our membership and in all that the group stands for—to the point that we're liable to be biased in favor of our group over others. This happens because our sense of security on various levels—e.g., physical, emotional, mental, or spiritual—is vested in the primacy of our group. In other words, we're liable to become dependent on our group for security and to help us get our other essential needs met. The price we must pay for what the group offers us is conformity to whatever the group requires of us.

Since all groups are created by and made up of imperfect human beings, every group is bound to have its flaws, errors, and limitations—be they minor or major. If we idealize our group for any reason, we'll be tempted to overlook or deny its errors or shortcomings, perhaps out of a naive sense of loyalty to the group. This is one way in which our need for intimacy/belonging may be distorted or exaggerated into an unrealistic and self-centered happiness program—that program being our membership in and identification with the group, and our desire to get what we believe the group may give us. Another way this may happen is if we expect or demand more from the group than it can possibly give us. This happens, for example, if we try to use our group as a *substitute* for personal one-on-one intimacy/belonging in relation to another special person in our life, our deep inner self, or God.

In some sad cases, rather than having our own personal action and relationships in life, we may be tempted to withdraw and live vicariously through our group and its star players, or at least the ones we admire the most—e.g., particular mass media entertainment idols, popular sports heroes, or political or religious leaders who are dominant in our group. In over-identifying with such public figures, we may try to fill in a gap in our private life by regarding the public ups and downs of their personal successes and failures as our own. We feel in our soul what we imagine is happening in theirs, and co-identify with it emotionally as our own personal drama. We may even co-identify with fictional characters in the movies and elsewhere.

This phenomenon of vicarious co-identification, which is healthy and normal up to a point, becomes unhealthy when carried to the extreme of using it as a substitute for living our own life. It may be seen at work in the tremendous emotional excitement, herd instinct, and group consciousness generated in political campaigns, religious rivalries, and mass media sporting events; and in over-identifying with the public accolades of the rich and famous. When we vicariously over-identify with particular individuals or groups, we may cease to live our own life and, as compensation, feel as if the victories and defeats of those others are our own.

At times, over-identification with a particular group and its views may cause us to stubbornly "dig our feet in," if we find our self on either side of a theological or other divide. Beyond outer group identifications and loyalties, our search for meaningful intimacy/belonging may turn to the arena of intimate personal relationships, where we have our own action and act in our own drama. Close personal relationships of all types are where most people seek and find, at least for a while, some degree of fulfillment in their need for intimacy/belonging. Experiences of intimacy/belonging in our relationships with groups or individuals may be real, imaginary, or a combination of these.

Most often, we'll seek friendship and intimate relationships with members of our primary group(s), who "speak the same language" because they share a common cultural, religious, or other conditioning and identity with us. This common ground is usually the easiest place to find a suitable intimate friend, since we already have some important points of identity, interest, and values in common with such individuals. Intimacy/belonging grows in a close personal relationship as individuals who are getting to know each other develop mutual feelings of fondness, caring, trust, and co-identification. A sense of belonging to each other as friends, lovers, partners, spouses, family members, and so on bonds them together as a shared "we," as opposed to each identifying more as a separate "me." As such a close personal relationship increasingly meets one's needs for intimacy and belonging, it becomes a firm basis for mutual empathy, commitment, and common ground between two or more individuals.

Growing intimacy/belonging in close personal relationships requires deepening levels of self-disclosure, trust, and vulnerability. One has to bring one's whole self forward into a close human relationship if its intimacy is to deepen and become authentic and complete. This can be a serious challenge in cases where individuals are fearful of the dark, rejected sides of their personalities. On one or both sides of the relationship, there may be conscious or subconscious fear of rejection by the other person if one's whole hidden self comes out into the open. Yet this is what inevitably happens as intimacy and love (God in us) reveal the truth of our soul. This is not done to undermine a close relationship but to make it more honest and real; and to offer an opportunity for healing of the wounds that are at the root of one's falsity and fears. If someone who loves us sees and accepts us as we really are, "warts and all," this can have tremendous healing power for the soul, and for the rejected, dark side of the personality. It makes the love between two or more people deeper, stronger, and more authentic.

Jesus said: "You will know the truth and the truth will make you free" (John 8:32). This great wisdom saying of Jesus has many important applications. Often we fear the truth because we fear that if our hidden truth is exposed, then we'll be rejected and lose the love of those we care about. Actually, the opposite of this is true, if they truly love us; and if we have the courage, humility, and trust to allow our self to be seen as we truly are in both our strengths and our weaknesses. This is the spiritual challenge of interpersonal intimacy/belonging. When we're afraid to take the risk of honest self-disclosure, once a close personal relationship develops to that point, then we'll be tempted to hold back, to keep up appearances; and we'll be tempted to retreat into the defensive shelter of substitute gratifications and a kind of pseudo-intimacy that prevents the growth of deepening love, creating an invisible barrier between us and the other person.

Then a close interpersonal relationship grows increasingly shallow and less fulfilling; and our soul's deep need for intimacy/belonging on the interpersonal level goes un-met.[3]

WHAT DO I REALLY WANT? WHAT DO I REALLY NEED?

We cannot be more honest with another person than we are with our self. Hence, meeting our need for intimacy/belonging inevitably has to take a turn within, in the soul-searching directions of deepening intimacy with our self and with God. Self-intimacy develops through honestly reflecting on our life and examining our conscience. "What do I really want?" and "What do I really need?" are two basic questions for such self-inquiry that we may continue asking our self throughout life. We may get to know our self better by observing our repeating patterns of thought, feeling, speech, and action, as we ask the above questions of self-inquiry. Perhaps the most profound question we may continue asking our self is, "Who am I?" Our answers to all of these questions will change as we learn and grow.

We are human beings with human wants and needs; and we are spiritual beings with spiritual wants and needs. Hence, "Who am I?" is a question of self-inquiry that needs to be answered on two basic, complementary levels. Our temporary human identity is determined by the circumstances of our birth and life in human ground; such as our genetic inheritance, physical characteristics, name, family of origin, cultural and religious conditioning, the groups with which we identify, what we choose to do, and the relationships and events in our personal life drama. Our human identity comes to us from our terrestrial ancestors, and it's what we and others around us see on the exterior and surface levels—e.g., our physical appearance and unique separate-self personality construction of ego-identity characteristics.

This, however, is not all that there is to us. If we think that it is, we impoverish our self needlessly. We all have a much deeper identity as spiritual beings created in God's "image and likeness" (Gen. 1:26–27). This deeper inner part of us is our spiritual identity and life in God. Full realization of our spiritual identity is ultimately the aim and potential of our soul's spiritual growth into the love of Christ. This spiritual growth of inner unfolding fulfills the promise of our divine inheritance from God, who Jesus teaches us to relate to as "Our Father." Calling God "Our Father" implies a preexisting relationship of intimacy/belonging on the deepest possible level of our soul's heavenly origins and divine potential. The Gospel of Jesus and teachings of the New Testament offer us the uniquely Christian path to the realization of this potential.

The harmonious integration of our human identity with our spiritual identity is the fundamental task of a mature Christian spiritual journey. This task of spiritual growth begins on the surface, in our human personality, and then works its way deeper into the soul's inner depths of spiritual ground. In order for this process to move forward, at some point there needs to be a recognition on the part of the separate-self personality in human ground of the soul's deeper essence in spiritual ground. From this point of deeper self-recognition forward, the inner work of the spiritual journey becomes a matter of bringing, with God's requisite help, the surface personality in human ground into harmonious conformity and alignment with the soul's deep inner-self in spiritual ground. The soul's deep inner self is both an individual and a universal identity at the same time (non-dual). The process of the soul's inner purification, healing, and transformation is accomplished by God's hidden presence and action in us through the gift of nonconceptual contemplation into which Centering Prayer leads us. The Method of Centering Prayer is but one of many possible ways into and through the gift of contemplation and this process of the soul's spiritual growth and inner blossoming.

When the surface personality is unable to discover or refuses to acknowledge the soul's deep inner-self and spiritual ground, then the tendency is to over-identify with the separate-self sense of ego identity in human ground to the exclusion of the deep inner self in the soul's spiritual ground. This inner divide happens because the individual mistakenly believes that the surface personality of separate-self ego identity is all that he or she has or is. It amounts to the loss of access to deepening intimacy/belonging in relation to self and to God, due to identifying with our temporary human identity in changing human ground to the exclusion of relating to our deeper, truer, more permanent identity in spiritual ground. Whenever this happens, the relationship with God—if there is one from our side—remains confined to the more surface levels while the most important and enduring part of our soul's identity goes missing. For this reason, over-identification with our temporary human identity and personality has been referred to as "identification with our false self," to the exclusion of our true self; and identification with our deep inner self in spiritual ground has been called "identification with our true self"—which is our integral true center and higher self in God.

The well known twentieth-century Catholic writer Thomas Merton (1915–1968) used the terms *false self* and *true self*.[4] They are modern terms for what Paul calls "the old self" and "the new self" (Col. 3:5, 9–10, 12; Eph. 4:23–25). The false self—also referred to as "the flesh" in Paul's letters—is simply a case of mistaken identity and spiritual ignorance that persists in all of us human beings to one degree or another until, by God's grace, we reach a level of spiritual maturity and intimacy/belonging in relation to God in which our true self is integrated into our human personality, and we've become more or less permanently identified consciously with our true self in union with Christ in spiritual ground. This process purifies, heals, and transforms our false self into an instrument or vehicle for the expression of our true self—which is our permanent and authentic identity as a spiritual being.

Like our true self in God on the deepest spiritual level, the false self is an essential part of our common ground on the human level. It's very important to appreciate this fact because virtually every human being has a false self of one kind or another; and all of our divisive misunderstandings and disagreements occur on levels of the false self in human ground. There are no disagreements or misunderstandings in spiritual ground where God's Will reigns and divine truth is intuitively known to all in the immediacy of the present moment. "The false self" is easily misunderstood as a pejorative term—which it is not. The falsity of the false self resides primarily in the fact that, in all of its diverse manifestations, it's a grossly incomplete and largely illusory idea of who and what we are. This is because, while acknowledging and embodying so many factual facets of our human-ground identity, the false self fails to grasp who and what we are as spiritual beings. To be human is to have a false self, and a true self.

"The false self" as defined above is a term accurately describing who we are as incomplete human beings—with the most important part of our total identity missing. Our total identity is our true self, which includes and *transforms* our false self via the sacred process of inner purification, healing, and rebirth in Christ. Until God's divinization process is completed in us, our false self remains as a relative combination of healthy and unhealthy tendencies. Our false self's spiritually healthy tendencies are those that align our human will with God's Divine Will and plan for us; the plan being that we freely choose to become a unique individual expression of God's divine image in our soul. Our false self's spiritually unhealthy tendencies are those that run contrary to God's Will for us in the forms of the self-centered emotional programs for happiness mentioned above, and the afflictive emotions of sinful, delusional tendencies that accompany and express them. The dark side of the false-self system in each person is the fear-based primary obstacle to her or his spiritual growth in healthy self-intimacy/belonging and in intimacy with God. Though some may insist on denying it, the false self is a necessary and inevitable aspect of being human. The false self constitutes one side of a critical psychospiritual divide in the individual drama, game, and life of each soul.

Each of us has our own personal Cross of unhealed emotional wounds and, consequently, our own unique version of the false self and its misguided happiness programs that are blind, unconscious attempts to compensate for those wounds. This is an essential, though mostly unconscious, reality of our common ground as human beings and spiritual beings struggling and suffering in the "fallen" human condition, where we do not often know who or what we truly are as spiritual beings belonging to God, our common Father. We are all fellow travelers in this human journey. The false self in each of us is neither all bad nor all good. It's a relative combination of flaws and virtues, of righteousness and unrighteousness. May the common ground of our individual false-self systems serve not to divide us, but as a new healing ground for mutual understanding, compassion, tolerance, and forgiveness in our individual and collective Christian spiritual journeys.

SHADOW DANCES AND THE DIVINE THERAPY

A chief obstacle that troubles the entire human condition is that we focus too much on our outer false-self differences in human ground, and not enough on our deeper unity in spiritual ground, where the same divine indwelling is uniquely present in each of us. Our common identity in spiritual ground is who and what we really are beneath the diversity of surface differences with which we may over-identify in the passing show of human life. We have ancestral roots in *both* human ground and spiritual ground. The former comprise our temporary human identity, and the latter spring from the holy ground of our soul's true identity in God. For peace in ourselves and in the world, we all need to outgrow over-identifying with our differences and under-identifying with our commonalities, especially the common ground of our inner unity in spiritual ground.

In this chapter, we've looked into our common ground as human beings and spiritual beings. On the deeper level of our spiritual ground, we have far more in common that unites us than there is that differentiates or divides us on the more exterior surface levels of our human ground. A key challenge to spiritual growth in our lives as human beings is to relativize our false-self human identity as we awaken to our inner life in spiritual ground. It's only through our soul's inner connection to God and the love of Christ that we may find lasting happiness, peace, and fulfillment; and the inspired vision to transcend all that divides us.

As we've seen, all human beings have the same basic instinctual needs as both human beings and spiritual beings. We are all subject to wounding in our needs, and to creating the same kinds of emotional programs for happiness as compensation for our unhealed emotional wounds. These unhealthy happiness programs exaggerate and distort the natural healthy expressions of our basic inborn needs; and we are all subject to the same toxic afflictive emotions that are triggered whenever our emotional happiness programs are either frustrated or gratified. This is universal common ground for all of us. Our childish happiness programs cause us all to become overly self-centered and over-identified with our human personality and egocentric separate-self sense—which has been called "the false self" because it's who we think we are but not who we truly are as spiritual beings created in the divine image and likeness. Over-identification with and attachment to our false self is the primary obstacle preventing us from freely accessing our life and more permanent identity in spiritual ground.

In addition to our sacred unity in the Body of Christ in spiritual ground, the false self in human ground is an important and essential aspect of our universal common ground as human beings. Every human has a false self. To say that one does not have a false self is the same as saying that one is "without sin" or error in one's thoughts, speech, feelings, and actions. As Christians, it's incumbent on us to humbly acknowledge our false selves and to be on guard against automatically acting out of our false self when responding to criticisms or interacting with people who disagree or oppose us. Only thus may we faithfully hold and live true to the Gospel values of love and forgiveness enjoined on us by Jesus. In doing so, we diminish the power and influence of our own false self while expressing our better self to others. Christ's love calls us to compassion and tolerance toward the false self in others as well as in us. I feel that this attitude, rather than one of rejection, denial, or condemnation, is a truly Christian and realistically honest approach to the "false self" in all of us.

The false self in any person is a mixture of light and dark qualities, healthy and unhealthy tendencies of Good versus Evil. In its negative shadow aspect, the false self comes from the wounded and unhealed parts of the soul that we've denied, rejected, and disowned because the pain, anger, fear, guilt, and other afflictive emotions tied to them were too much for us when we first encountered them. Consequently, these afflictive emotions and their wounds were repressed or pushed down into the unconscious, so we wouldn't have to feel them on the conscious level. Unfortunately, this "ostrich technique" of escape from the unwanted does not free us from it. Whatever is repressed into the unconscious ("the darkness" within us) remains active and alive down there in exactly the same state it was in when originally denied, rejected, and repressed by the conscious mind. There is no time in the unconscious.

What's repressed into the unconscious takes on a life of its own in the darkness within, and functions as a hidden adversary to the intents and purposes of the conscious mind. This is the origin of the false self in its negative shadow aspect. Something in our soul that's been wounded, disowned, and rejected is crying out in pain for recognition and healing. Perhaps our disowned shadow opposes us in order to get our conscious attention? If all else fails, pain, frustration, and suffering will force us to wake up! The healing of our false self's shadow aspect needs recognition and compassion from the conscious mind, to heal this inner divide in our soul. Bringing shadow aspects of the soul out of the unconscious and up into the light of conscious awareness automatically changes them. This is an essential part of the redemptive healing work of the divine action in us that Centering Prayer invites and that needs our conscious consent and cooperation.

As we read in 1 Corinthians 4:5, "[When] the Lord comes, he will bring to light what is hidden in darkness and will manifest the motives of our hearts." In other words, God's divine action in us will reveal us to ourselves by making what's unconscious in us conscious to us. This is an essential aspect of the "divine therapy" of

Centering Prayer and the gift of contemplation—revealing to us the truth of our soul.

What's in our unconscious is an important part of the truth of our soul. As we grow in intimacy/belonging in relation to Christ in us, the divine action reveals more and more of the truth of our soul to us, so that we may be freed from our unconscious obstacles and made whole in the love of Christ. This is another important application of Jesus' great wisdom saying: "You will know the truth and the truth will set you free" (John 8:32).

We are strongly tempted to act out of our false self when we feel threatened on the level of our basic needs for security, esteem, power, and intimacy/belonging. Confrontations with unwelcome oppositions across the theological divide may activate our false-self defenses—as we tend to have strong emotional attachments invested in the belief system of our religious faith, conditioning, and how we interpret it. In relating to a theological divide concerning our faith or prayer practices, we are challenged to abide in the humility, peace, and preciousness of our true self while honestly considering both sides of the divide. If we're truly secure in our faith, we won't feel threatened by conflicting views but will have the openness and curiosity to entertain all views with an eye to truly understanding the hearts and minds of those who hold them. Are we open to meeting such a challenge?

Fear and other afflictive emotions activate our primal self-preservation instinct when we feel threatened, and this easily motivates us to act out of our false self. Only God fully understands everyone's attitudes and point of view. This is because God, from God's side of Reality, is one with all of God's creation and each unique object, event, and life form in it. By God's grace, our common ground and spiritual identity in the love of Christ form the ever-present inner bridge across all divides of misunderstanding and confusion that may mislead or separate us from one another.

In caring human relationships, it's important to honestly and respectfully air our differences, whatever they may be; so that we may truly understand one another. In pursuing the ideal aim of peace, harmony, and unity among Christians and *all* humanity, our challenge is to remain true to the radical righteousness of Jesus' teaching of love and forgiveness for all. This revolutionary teaching goes against the grain of our separate-self common sense, cultural conditioning, warrior consciousness, and human reasoning. Christ's teaching is not based in the traditional practicality of our human-ground reality and struggles for survival; but springs from the higher, deeper truth, values, and perspective of our universal spiritual ground.

These two complementary perspectives (human ground and spiritual ground) reveal the dramatic contrast and divide between biblical "Earth" and "Heaven," between love and war in our human ground and relationships, and between duality and nonduality in our spiritual ground—where all differences are resolved. If, as sincere Christians, we're willing to take to heart our common ground with others as human beings and spiritual beings with imperfect false selves and God-centered true Selves; then we'll come to clearly see that love rules on the deepest level of truth in all souls; and in this light we may easily find the peaceful way to resolving all differences and bridging the divides that separate us from ourselves, from God, and from one another.

2

BRIDGING THE THEOLOGICAL DIVIDE

TWO OPPOSITE MODELS

The theological divide concerns our ideas about God and how we see ourselves in relation to God. It involves two completely opposite orientations to our relationship with God. We may think of these as the outer and the inner, as the extraverted and the introverted, or as the dualistic and the nondual. We may also view the theological divide in terms of rational theology versus mystical theology. In this and following chapters, we'll view the two sides of the theological divide as a thesis versus its antithesis; and the bridge resolving the oppositions between these two sides we'll view as a synthesis, arrived at by integrating their perspectives through the progressive stages of spiritual growth and our deepening relationship with God.[1]

In the book, *In His Spirit* (1982), Richard Hauser, S.J., introduces two opposite theological models that have been present in Christianity from its beginnings. Fr. Hauser identifies these two theological models as: 1) the Scriptural Model of the-self-in-God (and God-in-the-self); and 2) the Western Model of the-self-outside-God (and God-outside-the-self). Recognition of these two opposite theological models, and their far-reaching implications, is fundamental to Thomas Keating's conceptual background for Centering Prayer—which assumes the Scriptural Model of God-inside-the-soul and the soul-inside-of-God. There are several references to God-in-the-soul and the-soul-in-God in the Scriptures—e.g., "The kingdom of God is within [and among] you" (Luke 17:21); "I am the vine, you are the branches" (John 15:1–11); and "I will live with them and walk among them, and I will be their God, and they will be my people" (2 Cor. 6:16). Under the more binary Western Model of the soul-outside-of-God and God-outside-the-soul, consenting to God's presence and action in us—which is the heart's essence of Centering Prayer—does not make any sense, since God is assumed to be outside the soul (in contrast to present within it).

Each of these theological models offers us valid ways of relating to God at different times and in the different stages of our spiritual journey. What we're calling "the theological divide" develops when Christians identify in "either–or" fashion with one of the above two spiritual models to the exclusion of the other. This will inevitably lead to unnecessary confusion and misunderstanding, especially in cases where individuals are not aware of the two theological models and the fundamental differences between them. At first glance, it may seem logical to choose one of the models to the exclusion of the other because, on the surface, the two models obviously appear to contradict each other.

However, if we are willing to take a deeper look at them, we may discover that each model has truth and validity on its own levels of relating to God; neither possesses an exclusive monopoly on relating to God; and, seen in a broader developmental context, the two are actually complementary rather than exclusive of each other. If this is true, then it should be possible to build a bridge of reconciliation between these two seemingly contradictory theological models. First, we'll look at some of their differences and their origins, following from Richard Hauser's book, *In His Spirit*.

In the Western Model, our relationship to God is primarily an external one, since God is assumed to be outside the soul and the soul outside of God. There's an absolute divide between the soul as personal subject and God as an external object and all-powerful, all-knowing authority figure. Under the Western Model, the individual soul feels somewhat isolated from God, as one might feel isolated from a distant parent; and we experience a strong need to earn or win God's approval or favor; since the soul's future eternal destiny is believed to depend on this. If the soul performs well in human life, then there's hope of finding intimacy, reward, and love in its relationship with God. Human life is seen as a kind of proving or testing ground where Good versus Evil; and in which each soul earns future reward or punishment. It's believed in the Western Model that we're to initiate our good deeds, and that God is obliged to reward us for them in this life and the next.

This Western Model has roots in Western philosophy, from the ancient Greeks down to the seventeenth-century French philosopher and mathematician, René Descartes, who famously proclaimed, "*Cogito ergo sum*" (I think, therefore I am). This statement is Descartes' "proof" of the existence of the individual self and, as such, it affirms the existence and perspective of the human ego's separate-self identity apart from God. The Western Model seems to be a natural expression and outgrowth of the human condition's inherent duality of contrasting opposites. From this conceptual basis, which is confirmed by everyone's experience of human existence, it's logical to assume God outside the soul and the soul outside of God. The Scriptural Model, on the other hand, tells us there's something more and deeper to who and what we are than meets the human-ground eyes of physical sight and the intellect.

In the Scriptural Model, our relationship with God is primarily an internal one, since God is assumed to be inside the soul and the soul inside of God. There's only a relative divide between the soul as personal subject and God as an external object, since God is believed to be present in the soul and vice versa. Hence, there can be no absolute separation between soul and God. There is a preexisting familiarity and deep intimacy with God in the Scriptural Model, at least from God's side of the divine relationship where God's Word (Christ the Son) is present in all of us: "In the beginning was the Word...the Word was God...all things came to be through him.... What came to be through him was life, and this life was the light of the human race...the true light, which enlightens everyone, was coming into the world" (John 1:1–9); and "We are the temple of the living God" (2 Cor. 6:16). We are all God's beloved spiritual children, created in the divine image and likeness (Gen. 1:26–27); and as such, we each have a divine inheritance from God. This is the core teaching of the Scriptural Model.

We do not need to earn God's love, approval, or favor in the Scriptural Model because we are all already loved utterly by God with complete compassion and understanding. We have been given free will and are responsible for the consequences of our choices; but even our worst mistakes cannot diminish God's great love for us. God invites us into a deepening relationship in each present moment. We are always free to say "Yes" or "No" to this invitation. Likewise, God suggests to us what we might do to serve God's Will, and we are free to respond or not to these suggestions—which may come to us from without through signs and other people, or from within through our inner voice of conscience, inspirations of the Holy Spirit, or through our intuition.

The above basic differences between the Western and Scriptural theological Models of our relating to God may be summed up by such contrasting terms as *distance* versus *closeness, separation* versus *intimacy,* and *formality* versus *friendship.* These contrasts may be compared to the beginning stages of a relationship versus its deepening stages of increasing mutual familiarity, intimacy, and self-disclosure. Each deepening stage in the development of a relationship with God, our self, or another person requires correspondingly deeper levels of mutual trust, self-disclosure, and vulnerability. "Without trust, there is no relationship."[2] A searching question each of us may repeatedly ponder is: How much do I really trust God, myself, or another person? The answers to this determine the kinds of relationships we have.

EMOTIONAL FEAR OR FAITHFUL TRUST?

Another significant difference between the two contrasting models, pointed out by Richard Hauser, is that the Western Model—informed by worldly wisdom—tends to be distrustful of human nature, while the Scriptural Model—focused on our divine inheritance—is more optimistic and stresses our basic goodness as spiritual beings created in

God's image and likeness. This creates a significant divide of attitude and outlook between the two models. Both are true within the contexts of where they come from. That is, the Western Model, rooted in the perspective of duality and the pairs of opposites in human nature and experience, is correct in assuming that human nature is fallible and may be untrustworthy. This is undeniable, looking at human history and the present ongoing troubles afflicting humanity; and given, first, the psychospiritual compulsions and illnesses (mentioned in chapter 1) that hamper our human false self under the influence of fixations and unhealed emotional wounds in our basic needs; second, the conscious and unconscious emotional happiness programs that may take priority over moral/ethical integrity as they blindly attempt to compensate for our unhealed wounds; and third, the afflictive emotions that are activated in us and automatically acted out when our unhealthy happiness programs are either frustrated or gratified.

The tragedies of human history, relationships, and the current world situation—in which greed, lies, and corruption often hold sway—provide ample reason to be distrustful of human nature and intentions. This is especially liable to be the case when individuals ignore their conscience and live their lives without the inspiration and guidance of higher human and spiritual values. However, it's not always the case, in light of the divine presence dwelling in our souls—which is affirmed by the Scriptural Model, and which we may or may not consciously be aware of or relate to.

To the degree that the Western Model denies God's presence in us and teaches us to see ourselves as untrustworthy sinners who are unworthy of God's love unless we prove ourselves to be worthy, the Western theological model is liable to hinder our spiritual growth, engendering emotional fear in relation to God and self-doubts, guilt, and low self-esteem in relation to our self. This may lead individuals to reject and rebel against the Western Model (and their religious training) altogether, or else they may obediently conform to the model without questioning it and become overly dependent on external authorities and rules to meet their needs for security/survival/safety on the spiritual level. Under such conditions and beliefs, individuals may not feel motivated to seek a closer, deeper, more intimate relationship with God—who may be seen as a frightening and dangerous authority figure. This is a serious danger of the Western Model, when it is absolutized and taken too far.

The Western Model's distrust of human nature may carry over into our relationship with God; so that sincere individuals wanting to please God may distrust and fear the divine action's activities within them, should there be movements toward purification, healing, and transformation taking place in the soul. If God is assumed to be exterior to the soul, such movements within the soul are likely to be misperceived and wrongly interpreted by the ego or false self as coming from outside evil or malefic sources. Such distrust of the divine action may also be a form of resistance to change on the part of our unhealed human false self, which tends to be motivated by the afflictive emotions of deep-seated fear, doubt, and anger.

Under such circumstances, the theological divide between the two models becomes a divide between emotional fear and faithful trust in our relationship with God. Without trust, there can be no deepening relationship. This is why it's so important for spiritually aspiring souls to have a solid conceptual background regarding God's unconditional love for us, the Spirit's work in the soul, and the unloading of the unconscious (whereby toxic energies are evacuated from inside us so that inner purification and healing may take place in us). Too much emphasis on the Western Model's assumption of separation from God will deprive us of such a conceptual understanding of our inner spiritual life and God's preexisting love for and deep intimacy with each of us.

The Scriptural Model, in contrast to the Western Model, points to something holy, divine, and non-created in us (the indwelling Trinity) that somehow both transcends and integrates the limitations and separations of binary ego-consciousness, the false self, the Western Model, and created reality. The spiritual roots of the Scriptural Model are grounded in non-created Reality (God), which is nondual—meaning "not two," "not one in relation to two," but all-inclusive, allowing for everything, and without an opposite or equal. "Nonduality" is a tricky and elusive idea that may not be reduced to logic or fully conceived by the intellect. At best, humanly conceived concepts of nonduality may point toward its mysterious reality, which we may, at times, glimpse intuitively in graced moments. Ultimately, the mystery of nonduality and God is the mystery of Divine Love.

We cannot "wrap our minds around" these transcendent and utterly intimate truths of God and Reality; but we may, at times, experience temporary partial tastes of them as love manifests in our life and consciousness; through intuitive insights; and in radiations of the Divine Presence in our soul. Every experience of authentic love we encounter, regardless of how or where this sublime encounter takes place, is, in fact, an experience of God's presence and a glimpse of nonduality that takes us, in some degree, across the divide of separation. Such magical, spontaneous experiences—which always come unexpectedly—are the most meaningful, rewarding, and, sadly, all-too-rare experiences in our lives. They lift us to a higher vision of who we are, what the world really is, and of what we may become. Love, which brings everything together instantly in its timeless precious presence, is the ultimate nonduality. Hence, Scripture tells us "God is love" (1 John 4:8, 16). By Divine Love's non-created universality, which includes and upholds all unique individuality, we are all in God and God is in each of us. This is the shining ideal and core truth of the Scriptural Model as I understand it.

The roots of the Christian Scriptural Model in human ground come from the divine inner movements of the Holy Spirit that inspired the faithful prophets and scribes of the Old and New Testaments, when they labored to record in writing the Word of God as it spoke to them in charismatic experiences of the Holy Spirit, in dreams, visions, images, and the Spirit's tongue of flame alive in their hearts. The writers of Scripture also recorded faithfully, as best they could, what was passed down to them by word-of-mouth; but in the fresh language of a living faith that spoke through them as direct, immediate inspiration from the Spirit of Truth's living flame. The succeeding human roots of the Scriptural Model come to and from those who reverently read, ponder, receive, and interpret God's written Word and its deeper meanings through the grace of the same Holy Spirit Who inspired the original biblical writers. This process of inner prayer and meditation with the Scriptures is an ongoing transmission of divine light, life, love, and inspiration that's come down to us through the ages and continues unfolding in the hearts, minds, and souls of successive generations of Christians who open themselves in humility and faith to the presence and action of the Holy Spirit within and among them. According to the Scriptural Model's profound insights, we belong to God and God to us in a relationship of Divine Love and nondual, integrated Unity.

THE UNITIVE EAR, OR TAKE HEED HOW YOU HEAR

The theological divide with its troubled waters of division and disagreement arises whenever sincere Christians over-identify with one of the two opposite theological models to the full exclusion of the other. Such one-sided identification creates a kind of spiritual blindness. It's important to recognize that our human false self may identify with and function on either side of the theological divide, not only on the side opposite our own—so also may our true self of life in Christ. The theological divide gives rise to troubled waters of misunderstanding, mistrust, fear, anger, defensiveness, and even enmity when we act and overreact against one another out of our human false selves. This happens because our false self, on either side of the divide, may feel threatened if challenged by fellow Christians with different interpretations of the faith, and different prayer practices (ways of relating to God). That is, we may feel intimidated or threatened by fellow Christians across the divide who overtly disapprove of and devalue or doubt our personal religious views and ways of prayer and worship.

For example: people immersed in the Western Model, who see all souls as separate from God, are often unable to grasp the perspectives and prayer practices of contemplatives who believe God is in all souls and all souls are in God. Likewise, individuals who identify with the Scriptural Model may grow impatient with people in the Western Model who claim that the Scriptural Model's belief in the divine indwelling is heretical and contrary to the teachings of Jesus or the Catholic Church. There are obviously several workable theological perspectives from which sincere Christians may relate to God (who meets us wherever we are), interpret Scripture, and practice their faith. Whenever we judge others who seem different for any reason, we're probably acting out of our false self—especially when our judgment is lacking in empathy, tolerance, and compassion toward others.

We may read and interpret the Scriptures from many perspectives of our human false self, which is the everyday self that most of us know best and with which we habitually identify. As a result of this, the messages we find in the Bible are often determined by our habitually preconceived ideas, religious conditioning, and by what we're looking for; that is, what we see or hear in the Bible and elsewhere often depends on *how* we do our looking or listening. This psychological truism is perhaps why some critics of Christianity say that people may find *whatever* they're looking for in the Bible, focus on what they like, and then blindly disregard or ignore whatever else is in there. Thomas Keating has observed that when Jesus says, "Whoever has ears to hear ought to hear" (Matt. 11:15, 13:9), it is implied that there is more to his message than what we hear in its surface language alone.[3] He's trying to get at something deeper and intuitive that can't be reduced to spoken words and intellectual ideas. Our theological perspective and receptive openness are the human and spiritual "ears" with which we "hear" the message and meaning of Scripture in our heart, mind, and soul.

Our "ears" for hearing the Word of God may be attuned to any of the Four Senses of Scripture that are known in the Christian Tradition. These have been called *the literal, moral, allegorical, and spiritual senses of Scripture.*[4] The Western Model tends to favor the literal and moral senses of Scripture, which tend to be more rational than intuitive; while the Scriptural Model tends toward the allegorical and spiritual senses, which are more intuitive than rational. These senses of Scripture are complementary and offer us a helpful perspective for finding a two-way bridge of harmony, understanding, and reconciliation across the theological divide. The "outer" and "inner" may converge in relating to God and God's Word through the Four Senses of Scripture.

In the literal sense, the Scriptures are accepted at face value as historical fact and God is conceived of as being outside-the-soul and the soul outside of God—like a distant divine parent or authority figure overseeing His creation and always watching us. This perspective seems quite clear in the relations between God and the Israelites as portrayed in the *Torah* or Old Testament. The moral sense of Scripture concerns what God's Word tells us about right and wrong and how we're to conduct ourselves in human life in the struggle of Good versus Evil. The moral sense requires some mental interpretation of God's Word and of *how* we're to actually apply it in the practical living of daily life. Again, the Western Model's view of God-outside-the-soul predominates in the moral sense of Scripture, as we are faced with the responsibility of choosing between what's right and what's wrong in how we live our lives. A hint of the intuitive Scriptural Model of God-in-the-soul appears in the moral sense of Scripture with our discovery and recognition of the soul's inner voice of conscience.

The allegorical sense of Scripture reverses our focus of attention from external acts and what's outside us to internal choices and what's inside us. In this radical shift of focus, the Scriptures are internalized in such a way that *everything* in the Bible is intuitively interpreted as referring to the soul's inner spiritual life, past, present, and future, in terms of symbolic analogy. That is, the characters and events in the biblical stories are understood to represent different energies, experiences, and elements of the individual soul in the dramas and passages of its inner spiritual journey. On the allegorical level, the stories and characters (including Jesus) are about us and what we go through spiritually in our lives and relationships today.

All the disparate parts of the soul are represented allegorically in these dramatic biblical stories; our conscience, true self, Christ *in* us, our false self, dark side, human nature, happiness programs, and so on. Stories of conflict, oppression, bondage, communion with God, prosperity, peace, and abundant images of transformation throughout the Bible, all represent allegorically what happens in our inner spiritual lives. For example, the crucifixion, death, and resurrection of Jesus in the Scriptures may be intuited allegorically to represent our interior participation in Christ's Paschal Mystery; that is, the crucifixion and death of our lower self, or sinful nature, and the inner resurrection of our true self, or Christ's life, within us. This is a key process in the authentic Christian spiritual journey—which is more about becoming "a new creation" (Gal. 6:14–15) than it's about reward and punishment (as in the Western Model).

The Western Model may be present in the allegorical sense of Scripture, but the basic assumption of the Scriptural Model comes increasingly to the fore as we intuit that God and divine qualities are not only outside of us, but within us as well; as is everything that is *not* harmonious with our divine qualities and God's Will. The allegorical sense opens up a broad new dimension of personal revelation, relevance, and depth in the Scriptures that is quite unthinkable on the literal and moral levels of the rational Western Model alone. However, allegorical interpretations may become quite fanciful and do, at times, need to be balanced with common sense and a realistic appraisal of what's actually going on within us.

The spiritual sense of Scripture is the one that corresponds most completely to the intuitive gift of non-conceptual contemplation, where the soul rests in God, beyond thoughts, feelings, images, and particular perceptions of all sorts. This most profound and intimate gift of the Holy Spirit may be brought about in us only by the divine action in our soul. The Scriptural Model of union with God predominates in the nonverbal spiritual sense of Scripture. In this receptive, contemplative dimension, the Western Model is completely silenced and transcended by the Holy Spirit's immediate action in the soul.

This contemplative activity of God in the soul is the mysterious gift for which Centering Prayer prepares us. We are ready for this gift in our prayer life when: 1) we long for a deeper relationship with Christ, *and* 2) we feel called or attracted to quiet, receptive prayer by simply being or resting in God's presence.

The deepening movement through the Four Senses of Scripture, from the literal sense down into the spiritual sense, reverses the process that produced the Scriptures, gradually bringing us into direct contact with the living Word and Holy Spirit that inspired the original biblical writers in the first place. This process of the transmission of God's living Word through the Scriptures is an important part of our rich Christian Heritage. We may not be able to complete this process of inner transmission through praying the Scriptures if we restrict ourselves to the first two senses of Scripture (the Literal and Moral), and to the rational Western Model. The living transmission of God's Word in us needs an opening of our receptive capacity and spiritual intuition in humility and faith—which comes in the Scriptural Model through the allegorical and spiritual senses of Scripture, and the gift of silent contemplation that welcomes God's presence and action in our soul. Generally speaking, we need to go through the Literal and Moral senses of Scripture before we may penetrate deeper into the Allegorical and Spiritual senses. In this we may see how the Four Senses of Scripture may serve as a living bridge across the theological divide. All phases of the process are of equal value because, like both sides of the theological divide, they each depend on and complement one another in creating an organic whole in our human prayer life.

SEEING CLEARLY ACROSS THE THEOLOGICAL DIVIDE

It's usually easier for people in the Scriptural Model to see across the theological divide because they've already been on the other side in the Western Model (which most of us learn as children); so the Western Model is not foreign to individuals in the Scriptural Model as is the Scriptural Model to people who identify primarily with the Western

Model. The intuitive mystical insights of the Scriptural Model are foreign territory for Christians—whether they're laypersons, clergy, or even theologians—who've learned, know, and trust only in the Western Model and its interpretations. Hence, seeing clearly across the theological divide and bridging its troubled waters is appreciably more challenging and difficult for individuals who are familiar with and comfortable in the Western Model alone. For them, bridging the gap and troubled waters of the theological divide is a significant challenge and true Christian growth opportunity, inviting them to venture outside their comfort zones—which is where the Gospel of Jesus repeatedly challenges all of us to venture. Opportunities for Christian growth are there for all of us, if we're willing to open the closed circles of our preconceived theological perspectives, beliefs, and self-images, so that we may venture into higher spheres of greater, deeper, and more complete understandings imparted by the Advocate or Holy Spirit within us (John 14:15–17).

The deeper mystical understanding of the Scriptural Model does not negate the validity of the Western Model on its own levels, but integrates it into the Scriptural Model across the divide; so that the two may be united in a complementary unity of mutual respect and understanding that affirms the truth of both models and perspectives. The legitimacy of the Western Model is at least twofold: 1) it accurately correlates to our experience of life as separate selves in human ground who feel apart from God, i.e., our experience of existential aloneness/incompleteness in the human condition; and 2) the Western Model acknowledges and faces head-on the archetypal conflict of Good versus Evil in the human condition. If we're to make the false self true by honestly facing the reality of our situation and choosing the way of righteousness, then we may not "bury our heads in the sand" with respect to the limitations of our human personality or false self and the challenges we face in living lives of honesty, love, and integrity as human beings and spiritual beings in the drama and game of human life. The sincere pursuit of this moral, ethical, and spiritual focus is the Western Model at its best. We may fulfill the

Laws of Righteousness, as taught by Jesus and both the Western and Scriptural Models, to the extent that we are truthful and loving in our relations with self, others, God, and God's creation.

At its worst, and in addition to its previously mentioned dangers, the Western Model teaches a false-self Christianity that denies the deeper mystical truth of the Scriptural Model and conceives of "heaven" as a paradise for the false self in which its emotional programs for happiness will be fulfilled forever. The Scriptural Model at its worst becomes too other-worldly, denying the reality and value of this world, of the false self or any self, and ignoring the archetypal conflict of Good versus Evil in the human soul and the world. At their worst, both models are subject to self-deceptions and temptations of spiritual pride, self-righteousness, subtle ego (the deception of "no self" or "egoless ego"), and lack compassion for the sufferings of others. Whether either theological model is at its best, its worst, or somewhere in between depends on *how* it's interpreted and used. Both models are needed for a complete view of the human spiritual journey wherein God meets us wherever we are.

Meeting the legitimate requirements of the Western Model and avoiding its pitfalls are essential prerequisites for entering the way and traveling the path of the Scriptural Model that ultimately brings us into separate-self transcendence and Divine Union in the love of Christ. The spiritual journey across the theological divide is much more than a theoretical journey. The theoretical aspect may serve as a helpful preliminary for some souls, but it's not the actual journey of transformation into "a new creation" in the love of Christ. The actual journey is a journey of our self-identity and consciousness from duality into nonduality, from "I think therefore I am" into "I love because I *am* love." This "new birth" (see John 3:3–8) is the soul's ultimate freedom that completely fulfills our spiritual need for intimacy / belonging in relation to God, self, God's creation, and others.

A counterfeit "no self" (the self-deception of "egoless ego"), is often, but not always, conceived of in binary thinking as the opposite of a separate self. In this self-deception, (which may be its final hiding place) the false self plays at being "no self." Conscious human functioning always requires some kind of a "self." For example, in order for us to worship and adore God or anyone we love in created reality, there has to be some self-consciousness of separation from our beloved, as well as an experience of co-identity or union with or in the beloved. This wonderful epiphany of co-participation and co-identity with our beloved in the mystery of Divine Love is the astonishing, liberating discovery of nonduality that crosses, transcends, and embraces the theological divide, taking the awakening soul from the objective realm of abstract theory into the concrete subjective immediacy of direct firsthand experience. This is the only way we may truly know the hidden mysteries of God and the soul.

"Taste and see that the Lord is good" (Ps. 34:8). Only the grace-granted gifts of such personal discoveries of God's Holy Mystery in the soul may fully transfigure and finally convince the human ego or false self of the abiding truth and non-created Reality of Divine Love within and among us. It is the gift of silent, nonconceptual contemplation that brings us through this process and into this discovery—once the prerequisites as taught in the Western Model are being met and the heart is truly willing to consent and surrender to the Will of Divine Love.

The "no self" or "non-separate-self" that we ultimately are or become in God (Divine Love), beyond created reality, may not be conceived of by the intellect, expressed in words, or imagined intuitively because all such modes of expression take place within and are limited to created reality. As Paul reminds us in 1 Corinthians 2:9, "What eye has not seen, and ear has not heard, and what has not entered the human heart, what God has prepared for those who love him." Our divine inheritance holds the promise of more than we may possibly imagine.

3

FAR AWAY SO CLOSE: THE DIVINE RELATIONSHIP

GOD NEAR AND FAR

Two opposite ways of viewing the divine relationship we have with God are based on the Western Model and the Scriptural Model respectively. In the Western Model, the divine relationship is seen as one of distance, where God is believed to be mostly remote and far away. There are scriptural passages that support this view, such as Genesis 18:20–21, where the Lord God says that he "must go down and see" whether the behavior in Sodom and Gomorrah "fully corresponds to the cry that comes to me. I mean to find out." This Old Testament passage seems to clearly imply a gap of separation between God (as a limited individual consciousness) and God's creation; and therefore a lack of direct knowledge on God's part as to what is going on in God's creation. Otherwise, why would God need to take form and "go down" to Sodom and Gomorrah to "find out" what's going on there?

On the other side of the theological divide, the Scriptural Model tells us that the divine relationship is one of intimacy and closeness wherein the Divine Consciousness is privy to *everything* going on in God's creation. There's truth in each of these theological models, based on what people actually experience of the divine relationship; and they are not necessarily mutually exclusive. However, as we shall see, it's the Scriptural Model that ultimately points to the greater truth. As it says in the Book of Wisdom 11:26–12:1: "O Lord and lover of souls, your imperishable spirit is in all things."

≈

"Far away so close" seems an appropriate way to describe our relationship with God, since, in our separate-self consciousness as human
beings, God's presence often seems elusive, absent, and far away. Yet,
from God's side of the relationship, we are never separate or away
from the Divine Consciousness.[1] There is apparent separation only
from our side of the relationship we have with God. We generally
experience ourselves as removed from God's presence, as we perceive
reality from inside the bubble of our separate-self consciousness in
human ground. In reality, we are never separate or apart from God
because, as the Scriptural Model suggests, our souls are rooted in the
holy ground of God's divine presence, and everything that's existing
or happening in created reality is happening within the Divine Consciousness. Whether we are consciously aware of it or not, "Christ is
all and in all" (Col. 3:11). This is the revolutionary new perspective of
the Christian Gospel.

The Divine Consciousness has been fully present to and in each
of us individually from the moment of our soul's creation. Before
creation, there was nothing but God (non-created Reality). Out of
this nothing, conceived by God within God, creation has somehow
come forth into existence and continues within the Divine Consciousness—for there is and may be nothing outside of God or the Divine
Consciousness, which is absolute and infinite. Creation is God's self-
expression or work of art. We, as individual souls, are God's work
of art—created in the divine image and likeness (Gen. 1:26–27). As
God's spiritual children, we are very special to God and have, hidden
deep within us, a divine inheritance of love from God. This is true
because "God is love" (1 John 4:8, 16); and God intends for us to
share in love's perfection.

So, from God's side of the divine relationship, we are loved utterly
and completely by God. This is a great and unfathomable mystery
of God's infinite goodness—which is like an infinite pot of liquid
gold at the end of creation's rainbow (that is also its beginning),

a miraculous pot of living liquid gold that remains always full in overflowing abundance no matter how much is taken from it. There is no scarcity in God. Divine Love is God's gold and God is always so close to each of us, sharing secretly in all that we dream, do, are, and experience. Incredible as this may seem, God's loving longing is a divine yearning for each of us to know that we are loved by God— no matter what—and to realize deep in our soul that ultimately everything will always be all right, despite any and all appearances to the contrary. We may consciously come into this wonderful truth by discovering and becoming who we are as spiritual beings in the love of Christ.

Toward this end, God invites us into the divine relationship—so we may know and become who God intends us to be; that is, the fullness of who we are in God. We are always free to say *yes* or *no* to God's invitation. To say *yes* is to seek and ultimately find our way into the full truth of our soul. To say *no* is to lose this liberating truth and to become lost into the drama and game of our human false-self identity. Our human identity and personality is our false self because it is *not* who we are as spiritual beings in the love of God.

The difference between a human perspective and God's perspective is expressed well in Isaiah 55:8–9: "For my thoughts are not your thoughts, nor are your ways my ways, says the Lord. As high as the heavens are above the earth, so high are my ways above your ways and my thoughts above your thoughts." The ways of God are the ways of Divine Love. The divine relationship is about finding our way into our true identity as spiritual beings created in God's image and likeness. Toward this end, we may ask and ponder: "What *is* God's perspective?"

LEAP OF LOVE INTO GOD'S PERSPECTIVE

The divine relationship that we have with God is the safest, deepest, and most permanent relationship we may have. This divine relationship is God's own loving gift to us. To receive God's loving gift, we have but to grow up out of the childish immaturity of our human self-centeredness and unhealthy happiness programs; so that we may live true to the innate spiritual values of God's divine image and likeness in our soul. This is the basic challenge we all face in pursuing our continuing growth into the divine relationship. It's a challenge we cannot meet on our own without God's help. Hence, actively engaging the divine relationship involves entering into and sustaining a living partnership with Christ and the Holy Spirit's divine action in our soul. This is a continuing, lifelong process of human and spiritual growth as we live our life more and more consciously in relation to God within and around us.

We're always free to ignore or to acknowledge God's presence and the divine relationship. The development of our relationship with God depends on our ongoing response to God's invitation, and on the sincerity and depth of our willing and humble consent to the divine presence and action in our soul, which in turn depends on the priority of importance we pay to the divine relationship. How willing are we to really see and accept the full truth of our soul? God knows everything about us in intimate detail while we may see only a selective portion of our total true reality. For most of us humans, there are both light and darkness in us of which we are not consciously aware. Our soul is largely an undiscovered country of perils and promises holding love and fear, certainty and doubt, anger and compassion in the swirling energy field of its hidden mystery. Our deepest secrets are hidden from us within us by the automatic patterns of our past that persist in the present. Our loving God and deep inner self are fully aware of it all—but the false self of our conscious human personality and separate-self identity is not conscious of this truth and tends to doubt it when told about it.

The divine relationship is a course in self-knowledge imparted by God and leading us from falsity into truth, from bondage into freedom, from limitations into love. These are fruits of our partnership with Christ who brings us, step-by-step, into the freedom of the fold of heavenly love and peace beyond the logic of conceptual understanding. God calls us into a new life, a new way of being and becoming in the divine relationship that already exists and needs only to be consciously realized and embraced from our side of its reality.

Our side of reality in relation to God is the perspective of our human false self, which experiences itself as separate and apart from God—our holy ground and Source. As mentioned earlier, the "false self" in Centering Prayer's conceptual background is not a negative, pejorative term, as one may suppose. It's simply a realistic description and natural consequence of our being born human. The false self is essentially our incomplete human identity and personality apart from God. Hence, the false self could just as well be called "our human self." It's a temporary self, a changing mixture of positive and negative qualities that ebb and flow, like the tides and the seasons.

The false self is not all good and it's not all bad. It's from the perspective of our wounded and incomplete false self that we begin to relate to God, once we choose to do so. In the beginning stages of the divine relationship from our side, we relate to God out of our insecurity, unhealed wounds, and our self-centered emotional programs for happiness. The Divine Consciousness knows our heart and has great compassion for us, for *all* of us.

The false self is our temporary identity in human ground. Our true self is our eternal identity as a spiritual being rooted in God. The true self is all good. Since the false self is partially true and partially false (in the sense of authenticity and moral integrity), our job as spiritual aspirants is to work to make our false self true. As our false self becomes increasingly true, we grow closer to God within us. We need God's help for this to happen. That is, we may realistically make our false self become truer only in cooperative partnership with the divine presence and action in our soul—consenting to which is the heart's essence of Centering Prayer and an actively engaged Christian spirituality. The archetypal dramatic tension and divide between the human false self's perspective and the divine perspective in us is something of vital importance for us to meditate and reflect upon in the divine relationship.

Several examples of this archetypal tension in the divine relationship, and people's faith-filled responses to it, may be found in the Bible. For example: In Genesis 22:1–18, Abraham obeys when God asks him to sacrifice his beloved son, Isaac, perhaps the last thing he could have wanted to do; then in the Gospels we read, in response to God's requests: "May it be done to me according to your word" (Luke 1:38); and, "Abba, Father,...not what I will but what you will" (Mark 14:36). In the Lord's Prayer, Jesus teaches us to ask that God's Will (not ours) be done in us: "Thy will be done on earth as it is in heaven" (Matt. 6:10). Each of these examples, and several others, are presented as models for us to emulate in our inner spiritual life and the divine relationship we have with God.

There's an act of trusting surrender to God's Will manifested or pursued in each of the above scriptural examples. In each of these examples, the common-sense logic of human reasoning and separate-self interests are abandoned in faith and favor of an unknown future requested or suggested by God, either explicitly or implicitly. Such trust and abandonment are possible only in the committed depths of a divine relationship wherein one is willing to sacrifice one's own human preferences or agendas to those of the Divine Will present and active in the soul. The challenge is for us to go beyond reliance on our rational human faculties and our conscious understanding into an intuitive trust in the mysterious higher principle and power of Divine Love and what's promised us by God's Word (Christ) in the Scriptures.

From our human side, the divine relationship we have with God is a "faith relationship." Divine Love is absolutely true and infinitely real. Yet it's the reality about which we humans seem to know the least. Our faith relationship with God challenges us to trust and believe in the reality of Divine Love and its tremendous implications for us—regardless of whatever evidence there seems to be to the contrary in the drama and game of our human adventure. Our faith relationship calls our human false self to consciously remember that we're always in God's presence and God is always fully present to each of us. The discipline of this sacred remembrance of the One in whom "we live and move and have our being" (Acts 17:28), helps to balance our personal false-self perspective with whatever we may grasp, imagine or be given of God's greater perspective. The divine perspective is our unfailing Source of a blessed sanity and peace of mind. According to Thomas Keating, our participation in God's perspective in the divine relationship comes from the contemplative Gift of Wisdom active in our soul.[2]

We may not capture God's perspective by merely thinking about it. Such thinking is preliminary and secondary to actually experiencing something of the divine perspective. What's primary are the practice and development of certain contemplative attitudes that may open and allow us to experience little glimpses or infusions of the divine perspective into our consciousness. Some examples of these contemplative attitudes—which may be brought from our Centering Prayer or other contemplative practice into daily life—are: inner silence, solitude, humility, peace, preciousness, compassion, openness, and receptivity in daily life.[3] Slowing down into a contemplative attitude in the present moment creates inner space for us to receive and share in the compassionate presence of God's greater perspective—which is God's loving communication and gift to us in the divine relationship.

Our humble openness to God's perspective is an important practical aspect of growing in our ongoing faith relationship with God. The contemplative gift of our partial participation in God's divine perspective serves to show us firsthand how close we really are to God and God to us in the divine relationship—which often seems so remote and far away when we're identified with the conscious perspective of our human false self. Trust and faith are usually not easy for our human separate-self, which is haunted by conscious and unconscious fears, doubts, and insecurity coming from the afflictions of its unhealed emotional wounds. To compensate for these afflictive emotions in the soul, there is often a demand for reassurances, guarantees, certainty, and a sense of control in relation to the unknown. Such afflictive emotions are attitudes in which faith may not easily thrive and deepen. Hence, the afflictions and hangups of our human false self may keep us stuck in the more shallow levels on our side of the divine relationship.

In contrast to our understandable false-self doubts, Thomas Keating writes, "Christian faith is a leap into the unknown."[4] It is the bold letting go of our habitual false-self doubts and security blankets, and taking that "leap of faith" into the unknown where, beyond the threshold of our fears and doubts, the Spirit strengthens and supports us from within in our human encounters with darkness and uncertainty in the vicissitudes of life and death. As our faith matures and the divine relationship evolves, we move from habitual dependency on external things and reliance on our human false self, into a growing reliance and dependency on God within us. This challenging passage through uncertainty takes us again and again through passages of inner turmoil into prayer's peaceful waters that restore our soul (Ps. 23:2–3); into intimate depths of the divine relationship; and into a new freedom to know and become who we truly are in God.

GOD IS ALWAYS SO CLOSE

As suggested above, we may think of our eternal relationship with God in terms of the Western Model, the Scriptural Model, or in terms of some relative combination of these two—which is probably what most Christians experience in their relationship with God whether they realize it or not. In the Scriptural Model, where God-is-in-the-soul and the-soul-in-God, God is always so close as to be one with us from God's side of the divine relationship. Yet it may seem to us much of the time, in our human consciousness, like God is hidden or far away.

In the Western Model—where the soul is assumed to be outside-of-God and God-outside-the-soul—God is believed to be far away, even though, in the reality of the Divine Consciousness, God is always so very close to us as to be imperceptible—like an eye that can't see itself without a mirror, a nose that can't smell itself, or a tongue that can't taste itself. Perceptions in created reality always require a sensing apparatus capable of receiving and registering impressions; and perceptions require some degree of separation between the perceiver and the object(s) of perception. It's the same in any relationship, and it's only by God's grace and loving gift to us that we may sometimes consciously experience partial aspects or radiations of God's presence in us, or around us in others, and in God's creation. Whatever glimpses of God we may consciously receive are primarily manifestations of God's presence communicating to us in the energies and forms of created reality. They are touches of Divine Love's holy torch, but not the fullness of its living flame as it is in non-created Reality.

≈

God meets us wherever we are when we pray and try to relate to God. This is a key point for understanding the divine relationship and the diverse ways in which people may experience it, whether they regard God as being "far away" or "so close." The divine presence will relate to us in and through created reality on whatever level(s) we are open to consciously relating to God; and from there, God will invite us to move and grow deeper into the relationship. How the spiritual relationship we have with God develops depends on how we respond to God's repeated invitations, assuming we're aware of them.

We have three basic options in relating to God: 1) we may resist change and try to stay where we currently are in the habitual patterns of our comfort zone; 2) we may withdraw and regress back into more distant and superficial levels of relationship; or 3) we may take a leap of faith out of our comfort zone, venturing into new territory in our relationship with God and our self. The principle of these three basic options holds true in our human relationships as well as in the divine relationship. We always have choices to say *yes* or *no*.

There's a dramatic "risk–reward" dynamic that penetrates the progressive levels of a deepening relationship—whether it's with God, our self, or another person. As we go deeper into a relationship, there's increasing risk because deepening our involvement correlates to increasing self-disclosure and emotional vulnerability. Such risk-taking, if it's not naive foolishness, calls for discernment and increasing levels of trust on our part—that is, trust that the other party will not betray, exploit, or hurt us in some way. The reward connected to such risk-taking via self-disclosure in a relationship is the hope and promise of intimacy and love that may come from truly knowing another and being known as we truly are. Every authentic relationship is like a two-way street of collaboration that goes in both directions, not just one way. Both parties need to be engaged and involved, so that the self-disclosure, vulnerability, and trust become mutual and not one-sided. Only then may a relationship become truly rewarding as it grows into genuine equality, intimacy, and love.

Love unmasks us, exposing the truth of our soul to both us and the other person. In the case of the divine relationship, God already knows everything about us. So the revelation of our true reality will come as a surprise—sometimes an unwanted surprise—only to us, as the secrets we've been hiding from our self are revealed to us by God in the inner intimacy of the divine relationship. Unlike human relationships, where people may change their minds or fool us, there is no risk of betrayal via victimization or disappointment in the divine relationship. The difficulties we're liable to encounter there concern the inner purification and healing process in which we're challenged by God's loving divine action to face and accept the dark side of our personality that we've rejected, along with its unhealed wounds of fear, doubt, anger, and other afflictive emotions. Seeing our self as God sees us is a deeply intimate experience and gift.

Saying *yes* to the divine therapy of God's healing work in our soul—which reveals us to our self in new ways—calls for deepening levels of trust and risk-taking on our part in the divine relationship, as we're invited to drop the masks and illusions of our false-self defenses in order to go deeper into the truth of our soul.[5] The purpose of this divine therapy is to remove the obstacles in us that prevent us from actually living the Gospel values and growing closer to God's presence in our daily-life consciousness. Without a strong level of trust in our faith relationship with God, we'll not be able to let go and consent to the divine action in our soul as it discloses us to our self on deeper, more intimate, and sensitive levels; so that we may be healed and freed from the limitations and obstacles of our wounded false self. This process is a vital aspect of the inner work of Centering Prayer—which allows God to be God in us.

Each time a new level of falsity and afflictive emotions is exposed in the soul by the divine action, we're invited to die a little death in the heart of our false self. Each time we accept the truth and take responsibility for our unhealthy afflictive emotions, we experience the birth or "inner resurrection" of new life, freedom, and peace in us as the authenticity and intimacy of our inner relationship with God deepens and unfolds. This pattern of death and rebirth in the soul repeats itself many times over as we grow closer to God in intimacy, love, and truth in the divine relationship.

PERMANENT RESIDENCY IN LOVE, OR "HOW AM I PRESENT TO GOD NOW?"

Centering Prayer's conceptual background has identified four basic levels of deepening relationship that we may experience in human relationships, in relationship to our self, and in our relationship with God. These levels of relationship are: acquaintanceship, friendliness, friendship, and full intimacy or union of life. These four levels of relationship may serve as a connecting bridge between the Western and Scriptural Models of our relationship with God. They also correlate to the Four Senses of Scripture described earlier (pages 34–37).

The four deepening levels of relationship point to a graded conscious movement from isolation to intimacy, from separation to union, and from duality to nonduality; whether in relation to another person, our self, or to God. Since our human false self feels separate and incomplete in the absence of intimacy, love, and connection to our deep inner self, there's a great hunger in the soul for meaningful relationships, self-transcendence, and communion with Nature and creation's Divine Source. Individuals are often not fully conscious of what this great inner need and spiritual longing is, but we all feel its intense yearning in our souls. Hence, we often do not know where to turn to truly satisfy our longing for happiness, and to resolve our haunting sense of existential aloneness/incompleteness. As a result, we easily fall prey to the false self's emotional programs for happiness "that can't possibly work."

Human relationships and relationship to God are the two areas of pursuit to which we most often turn in our longing, hopeful quest to fill in the hole in our soul—which allegorically corresponds to Adam and Eve's expulsion from Paradise and the Lord God's presence in Genesis 2:7–3:24.[6] What we're all instinctively after emotionally and spiritually in our deepest desires and most important relationships, whether with God, self, or another person, may not become an enduring reality for us unless a relationship evolves into the fourth level (full intimacy or union of life), and remains there. So how does this come about? How does a relationship evolve from surface acquaintanceship into friendliness, friendship, and, finally, full intimacy or union of life?

Sometimes deep intimacy with another happens quite suddenly, as, for example, if we fall in love with someone or with God. However, unless we're spiritually mature enough and willing to give ourselves over to love and follow its lead, without trying to possess it and fit love into our self-centered agendas, the magic, wonder, and beauty of love's instant intimacy and fulfillment may disappear as suddenly and mysteriously as it came to us. Falling in love gives us a precious glimpse of heaven; but it doesn't make us permanent residents there, in that blessed state of consciousness. Falling in love shows us what's possible, what we're capable of feeling and being, if only we can sincerely believe in love's truth and humbly follow its lead in the attitudes of our heart. It's important to remember that "God is love, and whoever remains in love remains in God and God in him" (1 John 4:16). The great spiritual challenge for each of us, once we've found love or it has found us, is to *remain in love.*

Short of the instant intimacy and spontaneous feelings of fulfillment that falling and remaining in love bring, the normal course in the development of relationships correlates to the four levels mentioned above—each of which has several grades or degrees of depth. We may move back and forth among these levels and experience them in any order, in response to ongoing events and as the attitudes and openness of our heart change in relation to another person, God, or our self. In order for any relationship to grow, deepen, and evolve over time, positive choices and efforts are needed on both sides of the relationship—which is always a dynamic, creative, living, and collaborative two-way process that may change direction at any time.

Acquaintanceship is normally the beginning level of a relationship. It is preliminary or introductory and offers the lowest level of vulnerability, risk, or reward; since it maintains distance, objectivity, and requires little self-disclosure. Acquaintanceship is clearly the most common, impersonal, dualistic, and superficial level of relationship. It usually feels emotionally safe but offers the least amount of fulfillment or reward to the emotionally and spiritually hungry soul. Neutral topics (as opposed to personally sensitive ones) are usually discussed, and one relates to the other through the mask of a social *persona* that tries to be "polite, positive, and adjusted," according to the prevailing culture's norms and expectations. "*Persona*" is a Greek word meaning "mask" or "disguise." An individual's persona is her or his surface personality or "false self," the outer mask we present to the external world. On the acquaintanceship level, individuals tend to relate to each other exteriorly, "persona-to-persona," without going deeper. Hence, interactions on this level tend to be formal, functional, informational, and culturally conditioned; rather than personal and revealing of one's inner thoughts, feelings, and desires.

We all have literally thousands of acquaintanceship-level relationships with others in our lives, often encountering a person only once or a few times in passing. Acquaintanceship relationships tend to be "objectified," relatively impersonal, and unfeeling—though secretly, we may relate to others we casually encounter on any of the four relationship levels; that is, we may feel friendly toward them, empathic, or even intimate as fellow spiritual beings. Each encounter we have with another person is an energy exchange. When our relationships with others are limited to the acquaintanceship level, we're liable to feel isolated, lonely, and unfulfilled in them because our human and spiritual need for intimacy/belonging is not being met. We may suffer from interpersonal emotional starvation for lack of a meaningful sense of connection to others, God, or our self. Such lack of subjective meaning in our relationships creates emotional and spiritual poverty in the soul—for which we'll try to compensate by pursuing substitute gratifications or happiness programs—e.g., over-identification with our group or culture.

In terms of the Four Senses of Scripture mentioned earlier, acquaintanceship corresponds to hearing about Jesus and his teaching; and to the most literal interpretations of the Bible. God's Word comes to us through our various physical senses on the acquaintanceship level. This includes contacts with Nature and the appreciation and enjoyment of all our physical senses. In a person's religious life, acquaintanceship correlates to doing formally prescribed things on the external surface level, like attending church on Sundays, saying "grace" at meals, and reciting memorized prayers—such as the Lord's Prayer (Matt. 6:9–14).

Acquaintanceship prayer typically involves a lot of asking God for things that *we* want (i.e., "petitionary prayer"). If a person's prayer life is limited to relating to God part-time on the acquaintanceship level, then much of the time we forget about God and it's difficult for our divine relationship to grow into deeper levels of involvement, commitment, and intimacy. Acquaintanceship is at least some relationship, and it's certainly better than no relationship at all on our part. However, if we relate to God only at this beginning level, then the relationship will always feel incomplete and God will mostly seem to be out there somewhere, perhaps far away in the distance. Yet God is always present, close, and available to us, inviting us into deeper levels of prayer and relationship. So the question for each of us, at all times, is: "How am I present to God right now? How am I responding to God's ongoing invitation to intimacy and relationship? This asking and response on our part is, in itself, a deeper level of prayer.

The purely Western Model correlates to the acquaintanceship level of relationship because God or another person is objectified as being totally "other" and "out there," as opposed to being present subjectively and "in here" where we feel things. This sense of the self's separation from God is the root assumption of the dualistic Western Model of God-outside-the-soul and the-soul-outside-of-God. We all begin relating to God, or our idea of God, on this introductory level—as "out there," as separate, and as "other." Under this dualistic model, we tend to see the divine relationship as one in which God observes us from a distance and judges us based on our "good" or "bad" intentions and behavior. When acquaintanceship grows more familiar, it may suddenly or gradually move into the friendliness level.

The friendliness level of relationship is where we begin to take an interest in another person or in God, and where people start to warm up to each other. Human friendliness involves acknowledging and respecting the human and/or spiritual reality of another person to some degree. On the friendliness level, people choose to spend time together, getting to know each other as individuals, and sharing personal interests, likes and dislikes, opinions, and values. Doing things together is a universal way for people to get to know one another.

Relating on the friendliness level allows us to discover what we have in common with another person and where we differ. This is the level where people begin to reveal more aspects of their persona and to "feel each other out," so they may decide whether or not to pursue the relationship further. In friendliness, people begin developing personal feelings for each other and they think about each other when they're not together. Thus, in friendliness, people go deeper into their personas and start becoming engaged with each other on subjective feeling levels, as well as objectively on the external separate-self level of outer acquaintanceship. Friendliness develops as one grows to "like" another person, as opposed to disliking them.

When individuals on the friendliness level find that they share common interests and values, and experience a harmonious energetic chemistry together, they feel mutually attracted and are liable to seek a closer relationship. When individuals discover inharmonious differences in their interests and values, etc., then they're liable to back off from deeper involvement and perhaps take the relationship back to the acquaintanceship level. There are, of course, deepening degrees of friendliness and acquaintanceship; and we may change our mind at any time in a relationship, based on new discoveries and experiences.

It generally feels good to be friendly with people, especially when they're friendly toward us. Friendly regard from others is emotionally nourishing and helps us to feel good about our self; and less isolated than on the mere acquaintanceship level. Though friendliness involves some mutual sharing and self-disclosure, it's still a somewhat shallow level of relationship of one individual's outer persona to another's. Our persona is the mask we wear for the role(s) we play in the drama of life. In friendliness, we typically strive to "keep up appearances," avoid conflicts and too much vulnerability, and to limit what we reveal about our self. Hence, the persona does not always reveal what's really going on inside a person, but often hides or attempts to mask it. Friendliness involves a positive friendly attitude toward another person or others, but it lacks commitment, full self-disclosure, and isn't binding. Friendliness is noncommittal and preliminary to friendship—which, by comparison, is binding and involves deepening levels of faithfulness, trust, self-disclosure, and commitment.

On the friendliness level, we may relate to God in terms of both the Western Model and the Scriptural Model. Friendliness in relation to God is the level of mental prayer where we think about Scripture and interpret its meaning; we seek to act out its practical applications in our daily life and relationships. Friendliness corresponds to the moral sense of Scripture where we try to interpret what God likes and does not like, and to act accordingly. In other words, in relation to God on the friendliness level, we try to understand what God wants of us (as opposed to what we want) so that we may follow God's Will for us. Our motivation for doing this may range from wanting to stay out of trouble with God to wanting to do God's Will as an end in itself; because it *is* God's Will and we know (by faith) that doing God's Will is what is ultimately best for our own happiness, wellbeing, and fulfillment.

Our efforts to do what we believe God wants and to avoid what God does not want are basic practical expressions of our sincerity in wanting to pursue the divine relationship. This brings us closer to God from our side of the relationship, even when we're not successful at doing what we think God wants us to do. God knows our hearts and our limitations, and has great love and compassion for us, even in our failures. When God sees that we're sincerely trying to do what we believe is right, this counts for a lot and brings us closer in the divine relationship. As the Scriptural Model tells us, the inner motivation and intentions of our heart are more important than the outer actions we perform, in terms of the divine relationship we have with God.

Both the Western Model and the Scriptural Models may apply on the friendliness level. The Western Model acknowledges the struggle of Good versus Evil in the human soul and directs us to outer authority and formal rules, like the Ten Commandments, for guidance in our moral/ethical life. In contrast to this, the Scriptural Model, on the level of friendliness, invites us to listen to our inner voice of conscience, as well as to outer rules, in how we interpret God's Word in Scripture and apply it to our personal behavior and relationships. It's usually not difficult to bridge the conceptual gap between the Western Model and the Scriptural Model on the level of friendliness and in terms of the moral sense of Scripture.

Any basic Christian accepts that he or she has a God-given conscience, though questions may arise regarding how to interpret conscience and whether one is listening to a true or false voice of conscience. Inner listening is a basic attitude of Centering Prayer and the nonconceptual contemplation into which it leads us; as is consenting to the divine presence and action within. For people in the Western

Model, acknowledging that we have an inner voice of conscience may be a first step toward discovering the complementary validity of the Scriptural Model's teaching regarding the reality of God's presence and action in the soul. In the friendliness level of the divine relationship, we feel inwardly motivated to spend more than a minimal amount of time in prayer relating to God (as on the acquaintanceship level). Seeking direct contact with one's conscience via quiet inner listening may help to open the way within toward spiritual receptivity and the gift of contemplation—assuming one is aware and accepts that such a gift exists. The conscience is a voice of divine guidance and wisdom God has placed in the soul.

So, the idea of listening to our conscience may serve as a bridge for mutual understanding and reconciliation between non-contemplatives in the Western Model (where conscience is "formed" from without) and contemplatives in the Scriptural Model (where conscience comes from within)—especially when both genuinely care about growing in the divine relationship. Sharing the desire to grow closer to God, and acknowledging this common goal, may form a natural basis for mutual attraction, respect, communication, empathy, trust, and cooperation. This may happen if each party is willing to recognize and honor the sincerity of the other as a beloved fellow Christian who is not an adversary but a brother or sister in the Body of Christ. Such movement toward resolving differences is an expression of true Christianity, as advocated by Paul in his New Testament letters (e.g., Rom. 14:9–19, 15:7 and 1 Cor. 1:10).

With harmony and unity of purpose, and mutual respect regarding our common devotion to the divine relationship, we may share with one another what serves us in pursuing the Christian path of spiritual growth. Under such circumstances, what begins as mutual curiosity and friendliness may grow deeper into spiritual friendship. When this happens, our relationship with another person, or with God, evolves beyond the outer persona level into sharing the authentic reality of one's personal issues, cares, vulnerability, concerns, and deep inner self.

UNGUARDED EXPOSURE AND VULNERABILITY

When friendliness deepens, liking increases and begins to evolve into feelings of fondness, caring, attachment, and, eventually, loving on the deeper level of friendship. Friendliness on the persona level is conditional and often (but not always) depends on whether or not one feels attracted, affirmed, or in agreement with the other person. On the friendliness level, we may value others based on whether or not we perceive that they could help us to fulfill our self-centered happiness programs. Hence, on the human persona level, we often tend to see and judge others through the eyes of our desires, issues, beliefs, and separate-self interests. This is what often makes separate-self friendliness so conditional and contingent upon our personal preferences. That is, we consciously or unconsciously may use the relationship as a means to some end we desire; and our involvement in the relationship depends on whether or not we assume the other person (or God) can or will help us to get what we want.

All friendliness on the persona level is not this way, but much of it is when happiness programs of the false self motivate us. Whenever happiness programs are pursued unconsciously, the individual does not consciously see what he or she is actually doing and often assumes that something else is going on. When emotional happiness programs are pursued consciously, they take priority over the other person and the individual is consciously aware of and consenting to what he or she is doing. As we all know, sometimes, individuals will manipulate, lie, cheat, steal, and deceive to get what they want.

On the other hand, friendliness may simply be an expression of goodwill, compassion, or a positive attitude to others with no hidden agenda or strings attached. In any case, human friendliness always depends on the conditions that evoke it. Relationships on the friendliness level that are based on false-self happiness programs—where one person uses another to get what he or she wants—usually don't last and rarely evolve beyond the binary friendliness level; though there may be exceptions when individuals discover something deeper in each other to care about, and they manage to outgrow their unhealthy happiness programs.

When friendliness deepens over time, it may grow into friendship. The transition from friendliness into friendship usually happens by degrees, beginning as the liking or fondness of friendliness gradually moves from the surface persona level down into the inner being level of the soul; that is, into the soul's true feeling heart or center of meaning and value where we care deeply and where love resides within us. Love always changes our perspective from self-centeredness into something greater. We may think of entering this third level of relationship (friendship) as a gradual or sudden deepening movement in which our feelings and connection to one another travel from the soul's surface human ground down into its inner spiritual ground where we are touched and inspired by love and something of the divine perspective that love reveals and awakens. All real friendship involves honesty and engages the spiritual dimension of our being, whereas acquaintanceship and friendliness may or may not.

We generally relate to others *through* our persona in acquaintanceship, friendliness, and in friendship. In acquaintanceship and friendliness, we relate to another person primarily *from* our persona as well as through it. As friendliness deepens, we continue to relate to the other mainly from the persona level (the level of our human false self), but also slightly from the being level of our deep inner self expressing through our persona. As this happens, the relationship becomes more meaningful and important for us, especially if it's happening on both sides of the relationship. There's now a higher level of mutual self-disclosure, caring, vulnerability, trust, and emotional involvement in the relationship. We feel nourished not only in our personal need for affection/esteem/approval on the human level, but in our deeper spiritual need for intimacy/belonging as well. This deeper involvement has the power to bind us to the other person and to the relationship—which is something relatively unknown on the levels of acquaintanceship and friendliness.

Gradually, as friendship deepens, the extent to which we're relating to the other person from our inner being level increases; and the extent of our relating only from the persona's acquaintanceship and friendliness levels decreases correspondingly. If this deepening movement continues, at some point we'll be relating to the other more from our inner level of being than we are from our human persona. It's at this point that a friendliness-level relationship transitions into a relationship in the beginning stages of real friendship—though we may not notice it at first, since we're still relating to the other *through* our human persona. This transition is a significant change.

As a friendship grows and deepens, we'll still be in relationship to the other person (or to God) from our persona level much of the time; but the relationship will become increasingly grounded in the deeper level of being—where we experience and value the relationship more and more as an end in itself, rather than as a means to some other end or agenda of our human false self. As with all levels of relationship, there are many levels, depths, or degrees of friendship. As a friendship deepens, we come to identify more and more with the other person, so that how he or she feels directly affects how we feel. A palpable sense of belonging to or with the other person evolves, and we may adopt or integrate the other person's attitudes and perspective into our worldview. This can be quite transforming and may also occur in our deepening relationship with God; that is, we begin to identify with God's perspective.

Our shared identity and sense of compassion, or "feeling with the other," is a universal sign of the bond of friendship, which is a spiritual bond on the level of our deep inner self. We may feel this only in relation to certain special people in our lives; or, as we grow on the friendship level in our divine relationship with Christ, we may eventually come to actually feel compassion and co-identification with other people as members of the Body of Christ. Friendship on the individual human level takes us into our spiritual ground and prepares us for the greater, more advanced friendship on the universal spiritual level of the divine relationship, which reaches its full maturity in the fourth level of relationship, full intimacy and union of life. It's in authentic friendship and intimacy with others that we learn to love beyond the closed circle of our separate-self desires and interests.

Some of the deeper, more emotionally attached levels of friendliness are often identified with authentic friendship. This happens because practically everyone wants to think of some individuals as their "friends" (we all want to have friends), and the persona's deeper levels of friendliness may be as far as we're able or willing to go into a one-on-one relationship: with another person, God, or even with our self. Why is this? Though intimacy is one of the soul's deepest needs and greatest desires, it may also be one of our greatest fears. Intimacy and love expose us and bring forth the truth of our soul (that we may fear to face), and we may have unhealed wounds and unresolved issues that adversely impact our ability to trust. These factors may keep us from taking the risk of going deeper than friendliness into a relationship.

We may fear the unguarded exposure and vulnerability of going deeper into a personal relationship if we've been rejected or otherwise hurt before. Or we may not be ready to let go of our human persona (false self) and its separate-self agendas (happiness programs) to the point where we're willing to reveal them to another person, or even admit them to our self (God, of course, already knows all about them!). There's a certain sense of independence, freedom, and security associated with having our private world and separate-self sense; and we may be hesitant to allow anyone else into our secret personal world.

Entering into a personal relationship on the level of friendship (as opposed to friendliness) requires courage, trust, and willingness to take a risk, whether the relationship is with another person, God, or our self. This is because other individuals have free will to change their mind; to accept or reject us, honor or betray us; we don't know what they'll do; and we don't know what will happen to us, e.g., disappointment or fulfillment, happiness or heartbreak. We may be afraid to face our unresolved issues, and we may not trust God or our self enough to allow the divine action to reveal the dreaded secrets of our soul to us in the divine relationship. Taking the risk of willingly exposing and facing the truth of our soul is our price of admission into deepening intimacy with another person and in the divine relationship. We need to be willing to see the truth of our soul, for this is the truth that "sets us free" (John 8:32).

The above mentioning of risking self-disclosure and intimacy brings us back to the dramatic tension of the risk–reward dynamic that becomes increasingly active on each deepening level of any relationship; that is, as we venture into the unknown territory of the truth of our soul, and the souls of others we may come to know on the acquaintanceship, friendliness, friendship, or full intimacy and union of life levels. The greater are the risks of innocent trust, honest self-disclosure, and naked vulnerability to another, as we let down our defenses and a relationship deepens; the greater are the potential rewards of emotional and spiritual fulfillment in our soul's vital needs for affection/esteem/approval and intimacy/belonging. This dramatic risk–reward dynamic, and the uncertainty it brings, are at the core of every deepening relationship we may have: with another person, with God, or with our self.

BEYOND LONGING

The movement from friendliness into friendship is a deepening movement from our soul's human ground into its spiritual ground. Spiritual ground is God's territory in the soul. A different set of rules applies here than on the binary human persona level. These rules are based on the mysterious integrating nondual rule of love (God). The heavenly reign of God is the reign of Divine Love in the soul. This is an entirely different perspective than that of casual worldly relationships and our separate-self persona in human ground. Spiritual ground is the place of core relationships that transcend separation and duality. It's the inner wellspring of what's most meaningful, rewarding, new, and fulfilling in the life of the soul.

When friendship deepens, it leads into the fourth level of relationship: full intimacy and union of life. The rules here are based on the reign of God, the reign of Divine Love in the soul—which is nondual and unconditional. A good example of God's unconditional loving divine perspective is given in Jesus' famous Parable of the Prodigal Son (Luke 15:16–32).[7] God's unconditional perspective, as revealed by Jesus, correlates to the deepening levels of friendship and full intimacy or union of life—as compared to our more conditional human perspectives that correlate to the acquaintanceship and friendliness levels of relationship. In this famous parable of reconciliation and forgiveness, the Father (who represents God) loves both of his sons unconditionally. The two sons, on the other hand, blinded by understandable human guilt and bitter self-righteousness respectively, judge themselves and each other by the dualistic standards of human reasoning and the balancing scales of an-eye-for-an-eye justice. They fail to grasp the higher, nondual perspective of unconditional Divine Love—which we may intuit only by setting our culturally conditioned human perspectives aside, and by opening without prejudice to God's ideal loving divine perspective within us. God's unconditional divine perspective is that of loving everyone, no matter what.

The Father's divine perspective transcends the conditional logic of human justice and expresses the radical nondual principle of unconditional love and forgiveness—as was taught by Jesus. This wonderful parable has much to teach us about God's love, the divine relationship, and the need for reconciliation among sincere Christians who are divided and who bitterly disagree with one another regarding the true Christian faith. In the prodigal-son story—which tells us that ultimately our love for one another is all that really matters—we see the wonderful drama of healing, reconciliation, and forgiveness that comes to fruition for us through the inner spiritual process of repentance, conversion, and redemption in the love of Christ. It's our awakening into and full-hearted acceptance of the truth of our soul that allows this wonderful process to unfold within and among us. God's humble plea to us, the plea of the Father and the Son and the Holy

Spirit, is that we simply love and forgive one another. Love is the divine medicine for the spiritual ills of the human condition.

God is already relating and fully present to each of us on the deepest possible level from God's side of the divine relationship; that is, the fourth level of full intimacy and union of life. God's territory in the soul is our inner spiritual ground where, as the Scriptural Model tells us, *God-is-in-the-soul* and *the-soul-is-in-God*. This expresses the deepest spiritual essence of the friendship and full-intimacy-or-union-of-life levels of relationship. The fullness of these relationship levels of God's relating to us is always present, conscious, and active on God's side of the divine relationship. The Western Model of separation from God comes from our human-perspective side of the divine relationship, not from God's side.

From our human-ground side, we need—with God's help—to negotiate the passage of inner growth through our separate-self sense on the dualistic acquaintanceship and friendliness levels, down into our nondual deep inner self and true center of being; in order to realize the deeper levels of relating to God, our self, or another person. The fourth level of relationship between humans is realized as two souls grow together in love to become one-in-two and two-in-one on the spiritual level of being. Only love (God) may bring this about in the subtle silence of the soul's will and longing for love and union on the spiritual level. This consummation in love births a "new creation" that perceives God (the beloved) in all others—so that there really is no "other" from God's perspective (with which we become increasingly identified on the levels of friendship and full intimacy or union of life in God).

From the divine perspective, mystical self-giving and divine marriage manifest as selfless service and sacrifice in the spirit of great love and compassion for others (the beloved). In union with God, all others become the beloved. This is the practical and radical spirit of true Christianity as taught by Jesus: "Love one another as I have loved you" (John 15:12, 17). Everyone becomes the beloved and "there is no other" in the absolute sense of the term, because we're all united as unique individual souls in the nondual love of Christ. We're all inti-mate individual members of one spiritual family in God. This is the radically different perspective and rule of love that reigns in God's ter-ritory, which is the spiritual ground of all souls. Its realization com-pletes the soul's journey across the theological divide, where absolute separation (Western Model) is duality and Divine Love's integrating, transforming oneness that preserves and perfects individuality (Scrip-tural Model) is nonduality. We bridge this gap by growing deeper into the divine relationship.

FROM FRIENDSHIP INTO FULL INTIMACY

The friendship level of relationship corresponds to the intuitive alle-gorical sense of Scripture (where God's Word is internalized and interpreted as being symbolically about the inner life of the indi-vidual soul). The allegorical sense decodes and reveals the Bible's inner meanings for us individually, in terms of the soul's challenges of choice and the divine relationship. Our intuitions of the allegori-cal sense of Scripture follow from our faithful responding to con-science and to the moral sense of Scripture on the friendliness level. It's our humble responding on the level of the feeling heart that opens the inner intuitive way into new insights of self-awareness, intimacy, and friendship with Christ, where Scripture's allegorical mysteries and our hidden inner secrets are revealed to us by the divine action.

In the development of friendship with Christ, a process of grow-ing self-knowledge involving interior purification, healing, and trans-formation begins. This is the level of deep humility and spontane-ous outpourings to God that come from the heart. Music that really speaks to us may serve as a direct and easy way of connecting to this level of prayer. The Western Model of separation gives way more and more to the Scriptural Model of connection and oneness, as we engage the divine relationship and grow deeper in friendship and intimacy with Christ.

When we are moved from deep inside our self to long for God, to praise the Lord, give thanks, or express remorse for wrongdoing or sin, these outpourings are spontaneous prayers that come from the heart level of friendship in relation to God. True repentance, conversion, and forgiveness, with feelings and emotions deeply engaged, manifest on this level, where we are moved to want to change for love of God. Our growing desire is to become more and more what God intends us to be—i.e., our true self in God.

Prayers of adoration and praise, charismatic gifts, mystical visions, and inspirations of the Holy Spirit, when they occur, all occur at this third level of prayer or relationship to God, which we are calling friendship. When such things happen in prayer, however, they are not brought about directly by anything we do, but by the action of the Holy Spirit in us. For most of us, unusual experiences and phenomena are not a normal part of our prayer life. Prayer at the level of the heart, the level of feelings and friendship with Christ, may involve a wide spectrum of experiences, ranging from the very peaceful and ordinary to the sensational and sublime. Most important are the spirit in which *we* act, the motivation that brings us to prayer, and our actual attitudes toward God. It's our faith, humility, openness, receptivity, and consent that invite the divine action.

As friendship with God deepens, our inner spiritual life opens up and becomes increasingly important to us. We experience God's presence in us and the primacy of the Western Model simply fades away, like a memory of our time in exile apart from God's presence and intimacy within us. In addition to inner purification via humiliating self-knowledge and healing, the friendship level in relationship to God is where joyful freedom, relief, thanksgiving, heartfelt compassion for others, new life-giving energies, and insights into our relationships with others, self, and God awaken in the soul. As intimacy and trust grow on the friendship level, we begin to increasingly identify with and share in the life of the other person or of God.

The fourth level of relationship (full intimacy and union of life) corresponds to the spiritual sense of Scripture. The spiritual sense relates to the gift of *apophatic* (nonconceptual) contemplation (into which Centering Prayer takes us), and to the soul's nondual union with God in the love of Christ. It's in these deeper levels of the divine relationship (friendship and full intimacy) that we begin to directly access the soul's inner wealth of spiritual treasure—e.g., the nine fruits and seven gifts of the Holy Spirit.[8] The deeper levels of friendship and growing intimacy with God are beyond the scope of the dualistic Western Model to the extent that it regards the soul's separation from God as eternal and absolute.

The Western Model's root assumption of God-outside-the-soul and the-soul-outside-of-God is transcended and ultimately eliminated by the wonderful contemplative discovery of our life in Christ and Christ in us. Consequently, the divine perspective of the Scriptural Model in the deeper levels of friendship and on the fourth level of relationship (full intimacy or union of life) may not be conceptually understandable to individuals who relate to Christianity and to God completely in terms of the dualistic Western Model. It's in the deeper contemplative levels of the integrating nondual Scriptural Model that we begin to actually experience in us "the peace that surpasses understanding" (Phil. 4:7).

We need to "get our house in order" on the dualistic human level before we may enter into and abide in the integrating nondual unitive level. As long as we remain stuck anywhere on the dualistic persona level, we are not free to fully transcend our false-self identity and manifest our true self through our human persona. This movement of our human and spiritual growth parallels that of the movement from the human perspectives of the separating Western Model into the integrating divine perspective of the all-inclusive, nondual Scriptural Model—which is the true perspective of Divine Love.

In growing closer to God, the perspective of our human false self (persona) grows closer into harmony and alignment with God's divine perspective; and the motivation of our heart grows closer into harmony and alignment with the motivation of Divine Love (God's motivation). This is, I believe, what Paul calls our "new life in Christ":

"that you should put away the old self of your former way of life, corrupted through deceitful desires, and be renewed in the spirit of your minds, and put on the new self, created in God's way in righteousness and holiness of truth" (Eph. 4:22–24). This happens as the result of an inner transformation process brought about by the divine action in our soul. Centering Prayer is entirely in the serviced of this transformation process.

So, as we're brought deeper into our personal relationship with God, the Western Model's separation perspective gradually relativizes and, at times, disappears. As humans, we'll always feel some sense of separation from God, except in possible graced moments where the divine action brings us deep into silent union in the nondual Ground of Being and integrating Love of Christ. There's an interactive dance between the two basic theological models of separation and nondual oneness—and no end to our journey into Divine Love and the divine relationship—which moves from seeming to be far away to actually being ever so close. The following chart summarizes some of the ideas we've been discussing:

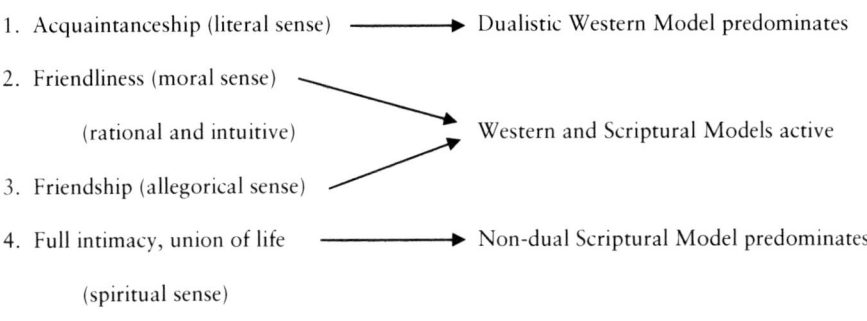

1. Acquaintanceship (literal sense) ⟶ Dualistic Western Model predominates

2. Friendliness (moral sense)
   (rational and intuitive) ⟶ Western and Scriptural Models active

3. Friendship (allegorical sense)

4. Full intimacy, union of life ⟶ Non-dual Scriptural Model predominates
   (spiritual sense)

Western and Scriptural Models,
duality and non-duality in 4 levels of relationship, senses of scripture

This chart may serve as a bridge connecting the Western and Scriptural Models. A bridge has its foundation on both sides of the divide it spans, whether it's across a river, a dry gorge, a relationship, or the conceptual gap separating two theological models of how we may relate to God and interpret God's Word. The Four Senses of

Scripture form an organic whole that corresponds to the four levels of a deepening relationship, beginning in acquaintanceship on one side of the divide and culminating in full intimacy or union of life on the other. Each successive stage of a growing relationship incorporates and integrates the healthy, life-affirming aspects of the previous stage(s) within itself, so that nothing of value is lost. Hence, the growth of our divine relationship with God is one of continuing expansion, inclusion, and enriching depths. This process of spiritual unfolding blossoms in the soul, leading us into increasing degrees of integrated wholeness and completeness in God, with our unique True self rooted in God.

4

The Gift of Contemplation and Centering Prayer

Origins of Contemplation

Centering Prayer is made for deepening our relationship with God. It's a simple method of daily practice that prepares us to receive the gift of quiet contemplation—which is the healing and transforming gift of God's presence and action in our soul. The heart's essence of Centering Prayer is consenting—or at least the intention of consenting—to God's presence and action in us and in our life. Contemplation deepens our relationship with God, and Centering Prayer is completely in the service of this divine relationship: that is, it's first and foremost a relationship with Christ and a discipline to foster the growth and deepening of that relationship. This is what makes Centering Prayer actual Christian prayer and not some other type of meditative practice—as some individuals may wrongly assume. By consenting to the Holy Spirit's presence and action in us, we are, of our own free will, giving God permission to be God in us and to do *whatever* God chooses or needs to do to bring us closer in the divine relationship.

Thus, Centering Prayer facilitates and deepens our participation in the divine relationship. It does this by creating the requisite conditions in us to prepare and allow us, by God's grace, to access the mysterious gift of silent, nonconceptual contemplation. This kind of prayer (that we're calling "contemplation") corresponds to the spiritual sense of Scripture and has its roots in the ancient Judeo-Christian Tradition. Elijah, the Old Testament prophet, is regarded as the "patron of contemplation,"[1] since, as subtly indicated in the Scriptures (allegorical sense), the Lord introduced Elijah to this new quiet, more intimate way of praying or relating to God, which involves listening to the divine presence within and around us:

Elijah had fled into the desert for fear of his life amid dramatic intrigues of treachery and the killing of God's faithful prophets. He was discouraged and depressed. Significantly, it was after "hitting bottom" and reaching a point where he was ready to give up his life and die, that Elijah was fed by an angel and directed to the holy mountain: "So he got up and ate and drank, and strengthened by the food he walked for forty days and forty nights until he reached Horeb, God's mountain," where he encountered the Lord in a new way; that is, in the simple, gentle quiet of "a tiny whispering sound" (1 Kings 19:8, 12–13). We may hear a whisper only if our hearing is close to its source. Previously, the Lord had mostly revealed his presence through dramatic demonstrations of mighty power and paranormal communications or phenomena—e.g., the Great Flood (Gen. 6:11–9:17), the destruction of Sodom and Gomorrah (Gen. 19:1–28), and Moses at the Burning Bush (Ex. 3:1–7). Elijah was thus introduced to a new, quiet, and more intimate way of relating to God—which is now potentially open to all of us.

Allegorically, climbing a mountain (which occurs at a number of significant junctures in the Scriptures) symbolizes rising into a higher state of consciousness. Elijah's ascending the mountain of God and being given an experience of the "prayer of listening" suggests that Israel, meaning God's people (which now includes *all* of humanity) were now being offered this new, closer, and more intimate way of relating to God in the divine relationship. The Lord, who'd been perceived as somewhat remote and far away, was now drawing closer to God's beloved children for communion and union in the mysterious silence of deep receptive prayer—which was first known as "the Lord's rest" or, in later Christian times, as "resting in God."[2] Though we can't place limitations on what God's mercy and grace may do, being at relative peace with our innate conscience (the moral sense of

Scripture) is generally a prerequisite for entering "the Lord's rest" (the spiritual sense), which is a sheer gift of divine grace.

There are numerous references to "God's rest," "the Sabbath Rest," or the prayer of quiet receptive attentiveness in the Scriptures that we may notice, if we're looking for them. One of the most well known of these is: "Be still and know that I am God" (Ps. 46:10). This is a concise formula for nonconceptual contemplation or the receptive prayer of quiet listening in silence. Some other examples are: "Rest in the Lord and wait patiently" (Ps. 37:7); "My soul rests in God alone" and "My soul, be at rest in God alone" (Ps. 62:1, 6); "Return, my soul, to your rest" (Ps. 116:7); "In returning and rest you shall be saved" (Is. 30:15); and in the New Testament: "*Come to me*...and I will give you rest.... I am meek and humble of heart, and you will find rest for yourselves" (Matt. 11:28–29); "Come away by yourselves to a deserted place and rest awhile" (Mark 6:31); "Let us strive to enter into that rest" (Heb. 4:11). These passages and several others from both the Old and New Testaments may be understood, especially in the allegorical sense, as pointing to the prayer of silence or "resting in God." The idea of practicing the moral sense of Scripture and following God's way as a general prerequisite for receiving the gift of contemplation is suggested in Psalm 95:11, where the Lord says of those whose hearts stray far from his ways: "Therefore I swore in my anger: They shall not enter my rest."

What *is* this rest—which comes to us from the Lord as a sheer gift? It's a blessed state of inner absorption into God's secret presence within us. Relative peace of mind is prerequisite for entering the Lord's rest. There needs to be calm in the soul, beneath the surface of consciousness, before we may go deeper within. The divine action may temporarily still our mind's habitual distractions and inner turmoil, in order to give us a taste of resting silently in God. This is one allegorical interpretation of Jesus' calming the storm at sea in Matthew 8:23–27, where the Lord's "sleep" represents resting in God; the storm represents the inner psychological condition of an unhealed soul; and the disciples' terror represents our human self's reaction to facing our hidden fears and unresolved issues. When the storm of emotional turmoil subsides by God's grace (Jesus "rebuking the winds and the sea"), and our mind resides deep at rest, then its waters are calm and we may abide in God's peace deep within.

Going through the storm of our unresolved issues (that we carry inside us) is an essential, repeating passage in the spiritual journey (as the divine therapy penetrates to deeper and deeper levels of the soul). Individuals who do not understand this inner process may misinterpret and fear contemplative prayer when their inner storms arise in the course of opening and consenting to God's presence and action within. Consciously encountering our inner storms is often an essential part of the soul's healing process. Thus, it's essential for us to have a firm conceptual background and understanding of the inner process of the spiritual journey, supported by faith and trust in the divine action of God's healing grace and mercy.

In the Book of Zephaniah, 3:17, we read, "The Lord...will rest in his love" (King James Version). Like the Lord abiding or resting in God's self as non-created Reality, our souls are meant to ultimately rest in Divine Love too. This same passage in The New American Bible reads, "The Lord, your God, is in your midst.... He will...renew you in his love" (Zeph. 3:17). Our soul's renewal, fulfillment, and perfection in the Love of Christ are the ultimate purpose or aim of the prayer of quiet resting in God. This is not something that we may bring about or do on our own; but, rather, it's something that God longs to do in us with our willing consent and cooperation. It may happen only on God's terms and in God's time. We are the humble receivers of this most precious gift in the divine relationship, and God is the most gracious giver.

The contemplative gift of resting in God deepens our participation in the divine relationship; taking it from devoted binary friendship (the level of full commitment and unconditional trust in God, no matter what happens), down into the deepest level of full intimacy and union of life in God—that is a completion stage in our spiritual journey which continues on from there into action in daily life. The journey of resting in God begins as we drop the surface mask of our social persona, allowing the divine action *"in our midst"* to draw us down deeper within our self, into a place of quiet humility, simplicity, consent, and trusting openness to God's unseen presence and action in the immediate present moment. Resting in God is an experience of silent inner absorption in which the divine action suspends our faculties of memory, intellect, and imagination as we sink into the quiet rest of a profound and subtle subjective consciousness that has no objective or reflective content. *Apophatic Contemplation* (contemplation without images) is the classical Greek term for this kind of prayer in the Christian Contemplative Tradition, which dates back to the early days of the Church. All other forms of prayer and worship, the more active ones we know and practice, are *kataphatic* (with images). *Kataphatic* contemplation—which uses our imagination and other faculties—is the requisite preparation for *apophatic* contemplation.

The journey through the many *kataphatic* forms of prayer and worship into the deeper *apophatic* dimension of simple silence and the Lord's Rest, creates a bridge across the theological divide between the Western and Scriptural Models of the divine relationship; as does our movement through the Four Senses of Scripture and through the four levels of our deepening relationship with God described in chapter 3 (acquaintanceship, friendliness, friendship, and full intimacy or union of life). As human beings and spiritual beings, we cannot be exclusively *apophatic* contemplatives. *Kataphatic* and *apophatic* prayer and worship complement each other, like a flourishing tree and its humble earthly roots—which are also heavenly roots grounded in God. We need the tree and its fruits, the binary and the *kataphatic* to connect us to our world. The forms of prayer and worship with which we are most familiar and comfortable are all *kataphatic* (with images); but they're not the only legitimate forms of Christian prayer and worship. There's something deeper and subtler that is needed to complete our journey into God. People who don't know this are liable to be distrustful of silent contemplation and methods that lead into it, such as Centering Prayer.

In *kataphatic* prayer and worship, our human faculties of mind, memory, imagination, and physical sensations may open us to divine grace and wonderful experiences of God's holy mystery; but they are fleeting and may never fully capture or contain God's Mystery. These passing experiences on the *kataphatic* level nourish our faith, keep us engaged in the divine relationship, and may move our hearts, minds and imaginations, uplifting, inspiring, blessing, encouraging, and comforting us; but they always pass and leave us longing for more of God's holy presence, love, peace, and overflowing fullness. To reach the intuitive fulfillment and consummation of our soul's deepest yearning, need, and desire, we must go beyond our limited human faculties into our soul's purely spiritual faculties of listening, love, and being—which include conscience and our non-binary integrating–transforming consciousness of love in Christ.

Silent contemplative prayer—which is God's great gift to us—is the most direct way into this mystery of spiritual communion and union in the Lord. It may happen only on God's terms and as a result of what the divine action does in us, with our willing consent and cooperation. We cannot say, however, that silent contemplation is the *only* way into transformation in Christ because God's great love, mercy, and compassion may freely choose to heal and renew human souls under any conditions, especially if we're truly willing to let go and trust God completely. Centering Prayer, in its humble consent, faith, and trust in the divine action, is implicitly asking God to do this work of transformation in us; and Centering Prayer creates a daily space in our life for this to happen.

Divine union in the love of Christ is the aim of Christian Mysticism—which takes us over time from being strictly binary Christians feeling separate from God, into the unfolding mystery of our divine inheritance in oneness with God. The contemplative path of Christian Mysticism may be right for us when we truly seek a deeper, more intimate and complete relationship with God, a loving relationship that moves our connection to God from being "far away" into being increasingly "so close." All ways of praying and dedication to God may contribute to our growth in the divine relationship; but it's the Lord's rest, God's subtle and mysterious gift to us within us, that brings us into our deepest relationship of communion and union in the Lord.

When we are in the state of deep rest in God, a state of true *"prayer in secret"*—which outwardly may resemble sleep but is not inwardly a state of unconsciousness—something intimate and profound happens between God and the soul in the hidden silence of the Lord's Rest. New energy and life are "breathed" into the soul by its divine Maker, initiating the mysterious process of inner purification, healing, and transformation—which gradually brings us closer to God and to our True self in Christ. This incredible process reveals the truth of our soul—including those parts we may not want to see—showing us the reality of our imperfect being in the intimacy of the divine relationship. Consenting to this process of the divine therapy requires deepening levels of humility, trust, and consent on our part, and willingness to give up some of our deceptive ego defenses, self-images, and the pretentious posturing patterns of our human persona or false self. In other words, we need to be willing to be stripped of our self-protective falsity and exposed to God and our self as we are in our unhealed human weakness and vulnerability. This process is a kind of ego death, and it's our inner allegorical participation is Jesus' Paschal Mystery.[3] This process of inner transformation creates the intimacy that will lead us into full intimacy and union of life with God in Christ. Hence, resting in God leads to resting in the truth. It means resting in and eventually realizing the whole truth of our soul with its flaws and impurities as well as its divine potential for completion and wholeness in the love of Christ. Resting in God teaches us humility, faith, and gratitude. If we're too attached to our human self-image, we may be unwilling to really let go and allow the divine therapy to do its work in us.

THE LORD'S REST

Let's now take a brief, deeper look at "rest," "the Lord's Rest," and the "Sabbath Rest" in terms of the Four Senses of Scripture. In Genesis 2:2–3, a well-known passage, we read: "Since on the seventh day God was finished with the work he had been doing, he rested on the seventh day from all the work he had undertaken. So God blessed the seventh day and made it holy, because on it he rested from all the work he had done in creation." Just think of it: the "Lord's Rest" of the "seventh day," in its deepest reality, is actually still going on throughout all time, creation, and eternity, balancing out the inconceivable immensity of God's unceasing activity that continually manifests and sustains created reality. Allegorically speaking, since we are created in God's image and likeness, we are invited and meant to share and participate in the Lord's Rest by entering, with God's help, into the prayer of silence or quiet rest in our true center of being and in the spiritual sense of Scripture. From a biblical perspective, the Lord's Rest on Creation's seventh and final "day" (which is still ongoing) is the ultimate origin or source of resting in God and of the Christian Contemplative Tradition.

In the literal sense of Scripture, "rest" is physical rest; God's rest on the seventh day is a ceasing from God's labor of initiating the Creation; and this is precisely the familiar literal interpretation and application of the Sabbath Rest for observant Jews and many Christians on "the Lord's Day." This is one reason why many businesses close on Sundays. That is, for many, observing the Sabbath or Lord's Day means having physical rest by refraining from all forms of physical labor or work. In their zeal for this traditional interpretation, the Pharisees even went so far as to challenge Jesus for healing on the Sabbath (Luke 6:1–11).

In the moral sense of Scripture, "rest" is the resting of our thoughts; and entering into the Lord's Rest is our participation in it as a result of seeking to align our self with God's ways in heart and mind. The Sabbath Rest in the moral sense concerns how we choose to spend our leisure time. Do we use it for worldly self-indulgence; for time with family and friends; for relating to God in prayer and worship; or for some combination of these things? However we choose to spend our leisure time, our inner motivation (the spirit in which we act) is always what determines the true spiritual meaning of our activity and rest in relation to God and the moral sense of Scripture.

In the allegorical sense of Scripture, "rest" is the resting of our feelings and emotions; and the Lord's Rest is something that happens within us, partially as a result of this inner calm. Resting in God in one's self is the inner allegorical meaning of the Sabbath Rest. It's free time we spend relating to God within and around us, so that we may enter into the Lord's Rest. In the spiritual sense of Scripture, "rest" means resting on the level of being. We practice the Sabbath Rest (any day of the week) most deeply by communing with God through the gift of silent, nonconceptual contemplation. Centering Prayer is a path, an open door into the Lord's Rest. Entering and abiding in the Lord's Rest in the spiritual sense of Scripture results in purification, healing, and transformation in our soul.

"STRIVE TO ENTER THAT REST"

This process of spiritual growth in "the Lord's Rest" has come down to us from the Hebrew prophets, patriarchs, and seers of the Old Testament. The Christian Contemplative Tradition has grown out of the earlier Hebrew tradition of the Lord's Rest or Sabbath Rest, and seems to have its scriptural origins in Jesus' famous Sermon on the Mount where, in Matthew 6:6, Jesus says, "When you pray, go to your inner room, close the door, and pray to your Father in secret; and your Father who sees in secret will repay you." This brief scripture passage is a primary source of today's Centering Prayer Method, and of our Christian Contemplative Heritage from its earliest days. Let's take a brief look at Matthew 6:6 in terms of the Four Senses of Scripture:

In the literal sense, the *"inner room"* is interpreted physically, as a private physical space away from others where one may be alone with the Lord. It could be a chapel, a room in a house, a solitary natural setting, a cave, a cell, or anywhere we may relate to God in private. This interpretation is supported by what Jesus says in Matthew 6:5, where he criticizes people who pray in public for show, so that others may see and admire them as being holy and religious.

Our motivation for praying is the basis for viewing Matthew 6:6 in terms of the moral sense of Scripture. Do we pray and practice other religious observances (like service or acts of charity) to impress others and promote our standing in the community, or is our primary focus of heart and mind on God, spiritual values, and the divine relationship? For most of us, it's often some combination of these two extremes. As Thomas Keating insightfully points out in *The Mystery of Christ* (pp. 38–39), our human false self, with its mixed motivations, can adapt to *any* role or activity we may engage in human life, including the religious and spiritual ones. On the literal and moral levels, *"praying in secret"* means having a private one-on-one time with God that is God-centered, and not self-centered in seeking affection/esteem/approval from others. Genuine prayer, in whatever form, is relating to God; and this may include relating to God's presence within us, around us, or in other people. Our inner motivation is always the key to the spiritual meaning of whatever we do or intend.

In the allegorical sense of Scripture, Jesus' teaching in Matthew 6:6 tells us to slow down, stop, and go inside *our self* in the present moment to pray. In other words, on the allegorical level, the *"inner room"* is inside us, not outside. *"Close the door"* is a metaphor suggesting that we disengage and let go of all outer distractions, and the inner distractions of our incessant self-talk and the random or focused productions of our memory, intellect, and imagination. To enter deep into the kind of prayer Jesus is recommending in Matthew 6:6, we also need a certain amount of inner peace and willingness to let go of our tendency to self-observation, so we may just effortlessly relax or rest into the simplicity of the immediate present moment—which includes and transcends *all* that is happening. Given the right motivation of seeking God in the divine relationship, and humbly consenting to the Lord's presence and action in us (which is the essence of Centering Prayer), this is how we "pray to our Father in secret" on the allegorical level. Centering Prayer is simply a humble method that helps us to do this.

"Prayer in secret" is prayer in silence; and it's also prayer in the unconscious. "The unconscious" holds all of those hidden areas, aspects, and activities in the soul of which we are not consciously aware.[4] Hence, we are not able to consciously "see" in us what "our Father who sees in secret" is seeing and doing, simply because it is unconscious and beyond the sphere of our human conscious awareness. In other words, "prayer in secret" is so secret that it's mostly secret from the person who is doing the praying! It's not something that we do, but something the Holy Spirit does in us—with our consent and cooperation. The real action of receptive prayer in silence takes place in the unconscious. We do not know what God is doing inside us in this prayer, wherein we become humbly receptive in faith, trust, and love, so that God may be active in us, doing whatever needs to be done to bring us closer in the divine relationship. Our job is simply to faithfully show up, give daily time to this mysterious process, and consent. The work of purification, healing, and transformation in our soul is entirely God's work.

The spiritual work of transformation God does in our soul as we practice Centering Prayer or nonconceptual contemplation is the "repayment" or "reward" Jesus refers to when saying "your Father who sees in secret will repay you." This repayment is a complex, paradoxical process that includes the "divine therapy" and "unloading of the unconscious." These are the necessary means the Holy Spirit uses to free us from our inner obstacles, and to bring us closer in the divine relationship. It's not always a pleasant process, and it's up to us to trust our divine therapist; even though we may not know or understand what God is doing in us or why. Trusting and willingly going through this process deepens our intimacy with God in the divine relationship, as we are exposed to the energies of the unconscious and confronted with the dreaded wounded parts of our soul that we've denied and rejected.

Each time we go through a round of divine therapy and unloading the unconscious, we grow a bit closer to God's presence in us, and some fruits of our divine inheritance begin to manifest in our soul. We may notice new feelings of inner peace, contentment, well-being, patience, and compassion for others as we begin to identify more with our spiritual true self, and less with our worldly human self apart from God. It's through this gradually unfolding process of spiritual growth that Christ redeems us to himself and we enter, by God's grace, into the divine life of our true self, the self God created us to grow up into and become. With time and patience, our life in Christ becomes a continuing reality for us. Allegorically, this is the outcome of our participation in the Paschal Mystery, and it's what Thomas Keating calls "the inner resurrection" of Christ's life in us. This "new birth" is the end product of the divine therapy and of our passages through the "deserts" and trials of unloading the unconscious. Union in Christ is the precious "repayment" eventually given us by our loving "*Father who sees in secret*."

DEEP DOWN INTO THE LEVEL OF BEING

Matthew 6:6, in the spiritual sense of Scripture, is our actual entering into the Lord's Rest via the gift of silent contemplation—for which Centering Prayer is a preparation. In the spiritual sense of the Lord's Rest, we go beyond Centering Prayer or any humanly created method or technique of prayer or meditation. The gift of contemplation is God's response to our *kataphatic* prayers of speech, reflection, devotion, longing, and imagination on the first three levels of relationship discussed in the previous chapter (acquaintanceship, friendliness, and friendship). Communion with God in the Lord's Rest is what all else in our prayer life was originally intended to lead up to. In the spiritual sense of Scripture (*apophatic* contemplation), God draws us into the prayer of full intimacy and union, deep down into the level of being, beyond thoughts, words, images, sensations, and all particular perceptions. Here, as we're immersed in the divine presence, a mysterious interchange takes place between God and our soul in the secret silence of the Lord's Rest.

In true *apophatic* contemplation, God is driving the car and we are in the passenger's seat. Our participatory movement from *kataphatic* (with images) activity into *apophatic* receptivity is a role reversal in our prayer life in relation to God. It means we are freely surrendering control of the prayer process and trusting the Holy Spirit (God) in us to do what is righteous, true, and necessary. This initiates our movement into full intimacy and union of life with God in the faith relationship. It's our evolving way from spiritual immaturity into spiritual adulthood in our relationship with Christ, as Paul writes of in his Letter to the Ephesians:

> Until we all attain to the unity of faith and knowledge of the Son of God, to mature manhood, to the extent of the full stature of Christ, so that we may no longer be infants, tossed by waves and swept along by every wind of teaching arising from human trickery, from their cunning in the interests of deceitful scheming. Rather, living the truth in love, we should grow in every way into him who is the head, Christ...put away the old self of your former way of life, corrupted through deceitful desires, and be renewed in the spirit of your minds, and put on the new self, created in God's way in righteousness and holiness of truth. (Ep. 4:13–15, 22–24)

This transformation of the soul in Christ is the aim of all true Christian Spirituality. It's what we all long and pray for as followers of Jesus, if we hear his words of love and promise in the core of our heart; and this transformation may not be brought about by our human self apart from God, but has to be the fruit of God's labor in our soul. The mysterious process of silently resting in God, consenting and ultimately giving one's self over completely to God's presence and action in us, is the "narrow way" (Luke 13:24) into this blessed transformation in Christ. It's the spiritual meaning of what Jesus teaches us in Matthew 6:6; and it's the reason for the development and continuation of our Christian Contemplative Heritage, of which Centering Prayer is one contemporary expression.

SECRET PRAYING

People living in biblical times and during the first several centuries of Christianity lived in a very different cultural and linguistic context than we have today. It was a world more different than we may easily imagine: There were no electronics, no printed books, no public education, and most people didn't have the opportunity to learn to read or write. There was no mass communication, and transportation was limited to basic physical means—e.g., walking, running, riding or being pulled in carts or wagons by domesticated animals, and rowing or sailing on the water. Human life was shorter, mostly localized, and its pace was much simpler and slower.

The Earth was thought to be the center of the Universe, with everything in the sky above revolving around it. Most religious teaching was done by word of mouth, and what was learned had to be memorized. People became acquainted with God's Word in the Scriptures and with the stories of Jesus by listening to them (especially before they were written down); and so it was with religious education, and learning the first Christian ways of prayer, meditation, and worship. Word-of-mouth was the primary vehicle for the transmission of spiritual teachings and early Christian lore. The documents of the New Testament were written down many years after Jesus' death, resurrection, and ascension into glory; the letters of Paul being the earliest writings in the New Testament, though chronologically Paul appeared on the scene *after* the events that are recorded in the Gospels had taken place.

That Christianity survived at all is no less than a miracle, considering how small it was ("*like a mustard seed*"), and the opposition it was up against from the Romans and from within Orthodox Judaism. How Christianity went from being a minor Jewish sect to a major world religion can only be due to the movements of the Holy Spirit in the hearts and minds of those who took to it in full faith, dedication, and commitment of their lives. Fortunately, the Holy Spirit had many willing and capable instruments through whom to work, such as Peter, Paul, the apostles, and everyone the Spirit inspired with the living faith and fiery energy of God's Word and the great good news of Jesus Christ within and among us. In spite of persecution and opposition from the reigning religious and political authorities, the new religion spread freely throughout the Roman Empire, like a windstorm of wildfire consuming dry sagebrush. After the Emperor Constantine (AD c. 288–337) converted in the fourth century, the Age of Martyrdom ended and Christianity eventually became the state religion of the Roman Empire.

As Christianity became secularized by becoming wed to the political and worldly power of Rome, there was a movement of devout Christians into the simple solitude and quiet of the deserts of Egypt, Palestine, Syria, and elsewhere. These people, who became known as the Desert Fathers and Mothers, were seeking intimacy with Christ through lives of simplicity, moral purity, devotion, and continual prayer. These Desert Fathers and Mothers were among the earliest Christian contemplatives concerning whom we have written records, though there were, no doubt, numerous Christian contemplatives from the time of Jesus forward. Anyone who deeply followed the Lord's teaching on prayer given in Matthew 6:6, in practicing *"prayer in secret"* on the allegorical and spiritual levels, would have become a contemplative, as Jesus himself, no doubt, was when he went off by himself to pray to and commune with the one spiritual Father of us all.

The earliest recorded teachings of the Desert Fathers and Mothers we have were compiled by a monk and ascetic writer from Southern Gaul of the fourth century named John Cassian (AD 360–435). In conference nine of his *Conferences*, Cassian quotes a desert father and disciple of Saint Anthony of the Desert, known as Abba Issac, regarding Jesus' teaching in Matthew 6:6:

> We need to be especially careful to follow the Gospel precept which instructs us to go into our inner room and shut the door so that we may pray to our Father, and this is how we can do it: We pray in our inner room whenever we withdraw our hearts completely from the tumult and noise of our thoughts and our worries, and when secretly and intimately we offer our prayers to the Lord. We pray with the door shut when, without opening our mouths and in perfect silence, we offer our petitions to the One who pays no attention to words, but looks hard at our hearts.

These words of Abba Issac give us a clear indication that some devout early Christians regarded Jesus' teaching in Matthew 6:6 as instructions for practicing *apophatic* (silent, nonconceptual, without images) contemplation. This kind of prayer has come down to us from Jesus' time through a continual succession of Christian mystics, practitioners, and teachers inspired by the Holy Spirit in both the Eastern Orthodox and Western Churches. Though most of this teaching was passed on privately by word-of-mouth (especially before the printing press and when relatively few could read), there is today a rich library of written and audio/video recorded documents tracing the history of our Christian Contemplative Heritage and Mystical Tradition.[5] All of this emphasizes deepening our relationship with God via direct, firsthand experience in prayer and meditation. Centering Prayer is an important continuing part of this living tradition—which needs to be renewed and updated in each generation.

TOO DEEP FOR WORDS

Beginning with Matthew 6:6, a number of methods leading into *apophatic* contemplation (mostly taught by word-of-mouth), have appeared within the Christian Tradition, such as *Lectio Divina*, the Jesus Prayer, Centering Prayer, and Dom John Main's Christian

Meditation. It's always a movement into simplicity; and into silence, into resting in the mysterious divine presence. It's a movement from various activities of our human faculties of memory, intellect, emotions, imagination, and physical movements / sensations; into the resting or quieting of those faculties by the divine action, as consciousness enters a receptivity of humble trusting silence wherein God becomes active in us as the Holy Spirit praying deep inside us with "unspeakable groanings too deep for words" (Rom. 8:26). These *"unspeakable groanings"* are the inaudible longings of God for the soul and of the soul for God.

Lectio Divina (Divine Reading) is an ancient way of praying the Scriptures and a companion practice to Centering Prayer. Its origins in Christianity go back to the times of the Desert Fathers and Mothers mentioned above. The *"four R's"* of *Lectio Divina* (originally a spontaneous process) are *reading, reflecting, responding,* and *resting.* The Latin words for these four moments of *Lectio* are *lectio, meditatio, oratio,* and *contemplatio.* We can see from the names of its progressively deepening stages that this process of praying the Scriptures is a movement through different levels of prayer engaging the faculties—e.g., verbal recitation, discursive prayer, and affective prayer, into the silence of pure contemplation or "resting in God" beyond the faculties. The four basic moments of *Lectio Divina* correlate directly to the Four Senses of Scripture and to the four levels of deepening relationship discussed in the previous chapter. *Lectio Divina* is one of the primary sources of Centering Prayer, which has restored the fourth moment (*contemplation,* or "resting" in God's Word) to the practice of *Lectio Divina.*[6]

Another well-known Christian Practice leading into quiet contemplation is called "The Jesus Prayer." This has been widely practiced in the Eastern Church. It involves reciting the phrase, "Lord Jesus Christ, Son of the living God, have mercy on me, a sinner," over and over again; first out loud and then silently in the mind. This may be done throughout the day as an "active prayer sentence." Gradually, it works its way into the subconscious and begins to automatically repeat itself.

It may also be used during formal periods of prayer or meditation. Eventually, the practitioner begins to subtract words off of the Jesus-Prayer phrase over time; until finally arriving at one single word: *Lord* or *Jesus*. Through this movement into simplicity, the practitioner will next be able to let go of the repetitions and move effortlessly into the silence of contemplative prayer and resting in God as the divine action draws her or him into it. This kind of method is more concentrative than Centering Prayer but ultimately leads into the same place; that is, the gift of *apophatic contemplation,* which is beyond all methods.

John Main's method, "Christian Meditation," is similar to though distinct from both Centering Prayer and the Jesus Prayer in its most simplified form. It's a concentrative "mantric" method that focuses on the word, "*Maranatha*" ("come, Lord Jesus"). The practitioner continues repeating "*Maranatha*" with heartfelt devotion and one-pointed concentration, until the mind slows down to effortlessly rest in silence. Then, the Holy Spirit draws the practitioner into the deepening levels of *apophatic* contemplation and "*prayer in secret.*"

LIGHTS OUT!

The gift of contemplation may be offered to us by God under a variety of circumstances, both within and outside our conscious prayer life—wherein we're intentionally relating to God. There's a high probability we won't recognize the gift of contemplation for what it is if we're not aware of quiet contemplation or "resting in God" as a legitimate way of Christian prayer and spirituality. Virtually all of the Church's mystics have been contemplatives; that is, prayerful receivers of God's divine action and rest within them.[7] If, during any type of *kataphatic* prayer practice—such as adoration, the rosary, reading the Bible, reflection, novenas, spontaneous prayer, charismatic worship, or reciting a devotional litany—we find our self wanting to slow down, stop and be still, not thinking of anything in particular; this may be an invitation from the Holy Spirit to enter into the deeper prayer of resting in God.

After an introductory presentation on Centering Prayer I was invited to give at a local church a few years ago, a devout woman with a very active prayer life came up to me to ask about an experience she'd been having lately that she said was interrupting her daily recitations of a devotional prayer exercise. She had a look of astonishment on her face and I think she already knew the answer to what she was intending to ask me—based on what I'd said during my presentation and a brief period of Centering Prayer we'd done. She was simply looking for reassurance and confirmation.

She was in the final stages of an Ignatian Spiritual Exercises Program and was doing a daily practice of visualization and recitation devoted to Jesus. In the midst of this wonderful prayer, she kept finding herself pausing from the prescribed procedure and sinking into a peaceful quiet reverie, in spite of her conscious intentions to do otherwise. When she came up out of this peaceful rest, she felt guilty and would apologize to Jesus for not being faithful to her prayer practice. "I thought you had to be doing something to actually be praying," she told me. Seeing the ironic incongruity between her earnest sense of duty to the *kataphatic* practice she was doing, and the Lord's inviting her deeper and closer into the intimate rest of *apophatic* contemplation, I felt a mixture of empathy and amusement at the same time. Touched by her sincerity and concern, I smiled, suppressing my inner laughter, and asked her to tell me more.

This "interruption" of her prayer had continued, in spite of her determination and efforts to stop it. She'd asked her spiritual director, the elder Jesuit Priest who was leading the Spiritual Exercises Program, about this "problem?" His simple and wise reply was, "Not to worry, God is putting you on 'automatic pilot.'" What a wonderful description of the gift of contemplation! He said nothing more about it. She continued to experience and be concerned about "automatic pilot" because she wasn't clear about it, hadn't been given any instruction regarding the gift of silent contemplation, and she continued to assume that you had to be "doing" something to really be praying.

After hearing about Centering Prayer and experiencing our brief period of it, she'd made an important connection. What she'd experienced in our group that evening was the same as what she'd been experiencing at home alone when her *kataphatic* prayer was being "interrupted" by "automatic pilot" and the Holy Spirit! I was quite pleased to be able to tell her she was being called to "resting in God" in quiet contemplation and invited into a deeper, more intimate relationship with her Lord. She, too, was quite pleased and amazed.

If people have not heard about silent contemplative prayer, like the good woman in the above example, then they may not be able to recognize this most precious gift as an invitation from the divine presence and action within when it's offered to them. Instruction in Christian prayer should include openness to the gift of silent contemplation and the methods (like Centering Prayer, *Lectio Divina*, the Jesus Prayer, and Dom John Main's "Christian Meditation") that lead into it. In contrast to experiences of resting in God that come during formal prayer times, there are also spontaneous experiences that occur outside of intentional prayer or any religious context. These are quite natural events in the life of any human being who pauses to relax and rest in the immediate simplicity of the present moment.

It may occur when one is communing with Nature, watching a sunset or the ocean, gazing into the heavens on a starry night; or simply lying down to rest, listening to relaxing music, or feeling peaceful and content in the presence of a loved one. Spontaneous experiences or hints of the Lord's Rest may happen whenever one is able to effortlessly relax and pause into the present moment. Since "God is love" (1 John 4:8, 16), and we are already loved by God as God's spiritual children, God is eager to invite us into the Lord's Rest; to share with us the divine light, life, and love of non-created Reality that may express into and through our human faculties of experience and awareness in created reality. It's all about deepening our relationship with God through the four stages of 1) casual relationship (acquaintanceship), 2) conversation (friendliness), 3) the inner communion of energies (friendship), and 4) union (full intimacy or union of life) on the level of being in Divine Love.

God longs to share the unimaginable beauty, goodness, and blessed fullness of Divine Love with each individual soul. This is the ultimate purpose of the divine relationship—which reaches its completion in the wondrous gift of *apophatic* contemplation wherein the soul is immersed and thoroughly soaked into the divine presence; integrated, impregnated, and reborn into the eternal light, love, and liberty of the living Christ. We come into divine union by being immersed again and again into the divine presence within us via the Lord's Rest and the gift of contemplation that gradually transforms us into "*a new creation*" in Christ.

Resting in God is a natural state for human beings to enter into, if we'll simply stop, relax, and allow it to happen. Resting in God is our natural state of being on the deepest level. If we'll allow our self to "rest in our natural state," and to be drawn by the divine action way down into it again and again, whether in a religious or secular context, we'll eventually come to discover our divine inheritance and who we really are as spiritual beings. As the author of the Letter to the Hebrews exclaims, "Let us strive to enter into that rest!" (Heb. 4:11)

≈

Since the capacity for entering the Lord's Rest is universal to all humans created in God's "image and likeness" (Gen. 1:26–27), no culture, race or religion may have a monopoly on it. Though it's referred to in different traditions by different *kataphatic* names and ideas, the process of entering the Lord's Rest is found in the *apophatic* contemplative depth dimension of all mature religious and spiritual traditions. The *apophatic* contemplatives and mystics of all traditions tend to understand one another, and to find common spiritual ground together far better than do the non-contemplatives in those traditions who focus on and are more identified with their *kataphatic* theological and doctrinal differences. This is pointed out by Thomas Merton, who met with a variety of non-Christian contemplatives during the travels recorded in his *Asian Journal* just before his unexpected and untimely death.[8]

Thomas Merton was an advocate for interreligious dialogue and his influence has sparked some valuable exchanges between Christian contemplatives and contemplatives of other Faiths.[9] The universality of what's called "the Lord's Rest" or "resting in God" in the Judeo–Christian Tradition is an essential point for understanding Centering Prayer's relationship to other contemplative traditions and its key place in interfaith dialogue. "The light of the human race...the true light, which enlightens everyone" (John 1:4, 9) has been present in all humans—at least as latent potential—since the beginning of the human family on Earth. This important spiritual truth is affirmed by the Catholic Church in *The Documents of Vatican II*, in the Church's "Declaration on the Relationship of the Church to non-Christian Religions" (pp. 660–674). It is also echoed in the *Catechism of the Catholic Church* (pp. 222–223, par. 839–843).

5

The Method and Process of Centering Prayer

Origins of Centering Prayer

In the introduction to his wonderful book, *Intimacy with God*, Thomas Keating writes about the origins of Centering Prayer and Contemplative Outreach. It was during the 1970s, at Saint Joseph's Abbey in Spencer, Massachusetts, where Fr. Keating was serving as Abbot, that the method of Centering Prayer taught today by Contemplative Outreach first took shape. It took shape in the context of a post-Vatican II environment wherein significant numbers of young Christians, many of them Catholics, were leaving the Church's pews, to seek a deeper spirituality and relationship with God in the contemplative and meditative practices being offered by a variety of gurus, teachers, and countercultural movements coming out of non-Christian traditions from both the East and the West—e.g., Hinduism, Buddhism, Taoism, Yoga, Sufism, Rosicrucian Philosophy, Theosophy, New Thought, Science of Mind, Western Magic, Wicca, and others. These young people were leaving the Church "in droves" for a variety of reasons, one of which was because they were unable to find anything to effectively feed their spiritual hunger for a deeper, experiential relationship with God within the parameters and practices offered them by the Church. They wanted something more and were determined to seek it.

Using our model of the four levels of a deepening relationship discussed in chapter 3 (acquaintanceship, friendliness, friendship, and full intimacy or union of life), we may say that many Christians have been inadvertently taught in their religious training to remain in the preliminary levels of relationship on the dualistic, separation-from-God side of the theological divide in the divine relationship. They've not learned about the possibility of a deeper, more intimate and imme-diate relationship with God through the receptive practices of silent *apophatic* contemplation. This has been largely due to the simple fact that those teaching them were not aware of this important possibility either.

Due to a pervasive anti-contemplative bias in the Church—stem-ming in part from the time of the Protestant Reformation; from nega-tive ideas and attitudes regarding human nature and the physical body (e.g., the heresy of Jansenism); and from the tragically false notion that silent contemplation is a rare gift reserved for only the most holy and saintly people—many monks, priests, and nuns both inside and outside of monasteries were neither educated about nor interested in *apophatic* contemplative prayer. Those charged with teaching others about Christian prayer and spirituality couldn't effectively teach what they felt they were unworthy of or didn't know anything substantial about themselves. There were, of course, some notable exceptions to this, e.g., contemplative orders like the Discalced Carmelites and the Carthusians; and, within the Cistercian (Trappist) Order, Frs. Thomas Merton, William Meninger, Thomas Keating, and Basil Pennington— the chief architects and inspirers of Centering Prayer.[1]

The actual method of Centering Prayer comes directly out of the anonymous fourteenth-century Christian contemplative classic, *The Cloud of Unknowing*. Fr. William Meninger, a Bible scholar and avid student of pre-sixteenth-century Christian spirituality, happened one day to discover a dusty old copy of *The Cloud of Unknowing*, writ-ten in Middle English, in the library of Saint Joseph's Abbey, where he was a monk at the time. This was in the early 1970s. Fr. William, who'd felt drawn to "loving God in silence," was quite taken with the book; and from it he developed the beginnings of the Centering Prayer Method—which, he's said, "could just as well have been called 'The Prayer of the Cloud.'"[2] Aware of the immense value of silent con-templation and "resting in God" for deepening our experience of the divine relationship, and of the dearth of practical instruction in this kind of prayer offered to priests and religious in the Seminaries and

Convents, Fr. William began offering instruction and silent retreats in "the Prayer of the Cloud" to local clergy and religious in the guest-house at the Abbey. Some wondered about what they were doing, but the response was very positive from those who took to this prayer. At some later point, the decision was made to call this simple prayer method "Centering Prayer," a term Thomas Merton had inspired.

One priest who took to this new–old way of quiet prayer was Fr. Carl J. Arico, from the Diocese of Newark, New Jersey. The discovery of silent contemplative prayer was a watershed cathartic event in Fr. Carl's spiritual and priestly life. Two significant comments I've heard him make regarding this are something like: "When I discovered the treasure of Centering Prayer, my soul was greatly enriched, it was a wonderful new beginning for me in deepening my relationship with God; but I also felt like I'd been cheated by my training in Christian spirituality in the Seminary because they never told us about this!" A second statement Fr. Carl has made is, "I went up the hill to that retreat at Saint Joseph's Abbey as Carl the Priest; I came back down as Carl the human being who happens to be a Priest." He'd experienced an important shift in his perspective and identity as a human being and a spiritual being through his practice of Centering Prayer and the gift of *apophatic* contemplation. With special permission from his Bishop, Fr. Carl has devoted over thirty years of his life full-time to teaching and sharing Centering Prayer and the Christian Spiritual Journey with others.

OLD TREASURE

Abbot Keating took a keen interest in Fr. William's contemplative retreats; and so did Fr. Basil Pennington, who also was a Trappist monk at Saint Joseph's Abbey. Fr. Basil has said that he "learned contemplative prayer from my grandmother." With the involvement of these three monks and priests, who'd dedicated their lives to the Gospel of Jesus, the Church, and to the study, practice, and teaching of Christian spirituality—especially in its *apophatic* dimension as taught in *The Cloud of Unknowing* and elsewhere—the Method of Centering Prayer was born and took shape. Each of the three had their own way of teaching it: Fr. William teaching from *The Cloud of Unknowing*; Fr. Basil from the Gospels; and Fr. Thomas offering the Centering Prayer Method as presented in *Open Mind, Open Heart* and in Contemplative Outreach's Centering Prayer Brochure (see below).

Noticing the success of the how-to methods and techniques of meditation being offered in the West by Eastern gurus and teachers, they were looking for a simple, practical way to distill, package, and present the essence of the Christian Contemplative Tradition that would be suitable for contemporary people living modern lifestyles. They knew a former monk who was teaching Transcendental Meditation; and, in the spirit of interreligious dialogue, Abbot Keating invited a local Zen *Roshi* (accomplished teacher) to lead his monks in a weeklong *Sessin* (sitting meditation practice retreat). These two simple examples provided workable structures for packaging the Centering Prayer Method for daily practice, and for organizing intensive Christian contemplative practice retreats using the Centering Prayer Method. The outer form or "packaging" was similar to TM and Zen, but the contents and intention of Centering Prayer were completely Christian; that is, the theological focus of Centering Prayer is on consenting to the presence and action in the soul of the divine indwelling of Father, Son, and Holy Spirit; and traditional *kataphatic* elements of Christian prayer and worship (e.g., Psalm reading, Mass, *Lectio Divina*), based on Christian Monastic Spirituality, were built around daily Centering Prayer practice and incorporated into the retreats.

The setting and "vestibule" for entering into private Centering Prayer practice, which may include, for example, Scripture reading, petitionary prayer, mental prayer or affective prayer, is left to the discretion and free choice of the individual practitioner. Some typical examples found at Centering Prayer retreats include: silence; spiritual reading at meals (usually from Thomas Keating's foundational book on Centering Prayer, *Open Mind, Open Heart*); daily Mass and Eucharist; *Lectio Divina*: spiritual talks in a live or video format;

private conferences with retreat staff; and Psalm reading prior to communal Centering Prayer sessions. It's the *kataphatic* elements that create the particularly Christian atmosphere and character of these silent Centering Prayer retreats—which may last anywhere from a weekend up to ten days. For more about the silence at these retreats, see Appendix One, on "Silence and Solitude."

The actual Method of Centering Prayer, as taught by Thomas Keating and Contemplative Outreach, has Four Basic Guidelines: "1. Choose a sacred word as the symbol of your intention to consent to God's presence and action within; 2. Sitting comfortably with eyes closed, settle briefly and silently introduce the sacred word as the symbol of your consent to God's presence and action within; 3. When engaged with your thoughts (including bodily sensations, feelings, images, and reflections), return ever so gently to the sacred word; 4. At the end of the prayer period, remain in silence with eyes closed for a couple of minutes."[3]

These guidelines for Centering Prayer practice are developed in the Contemplative Outreach brochure, "The Method of Centering Prayer: The Prayer of Consent." They are nuanced and discussed in further detail in a number of excellent books and videos on the method of Centering Prayer,[4] which was developed because its founders, Frs. Meninger, Keating, and Pennington wanted to offer "a Christian alternative to people going to the East" for a deeper spirituality. They realized there was "a lack of a way of teaching contemplative prayer" to both professed religious with active ministries and lay persons living active lives in contemporary society. The "how-to" method of Centering Prayer and its conceptual background (which is essential for understanding the inner spiritual process of Centering Prayer), are adapted to the times and conditions in which we are now living.

Experience teaches us that we can't always know what someone or something is really like on the inside merely on the basis of how he, she, or it appears to us on the outside. This is true with people and it's also true with spiritual practices, like Centering Prayer. A very wise man from the East once said: "Accept nothing that is unreasonable; and reject nothing as being unreasonable without proper examination." This certainly applies regarding Centering Prayer and those who misunderstand what it really is as a Christian spiritual practice and way of deepening our relationship with God. As in all relationships, trust is the critical factor in our openness to one another or to anything important that we may choose to look into. Without trust, there may be no deep or meaningful relationship beyond the surface level.

One of the chief objections to Centering Prayer is the mistaken claim that it's really Eastern Religion or Transcendental Meditation dressed up in a "Christian disguise." This confusion is understandable for individuals, like many sincere Christians, who do not know very much about the Christian Contemplative Tradition because they've never had an opportunity to study or practice it in any depth. One of the purposes of the Centering Prayer movement is to remedy this situation by renewing the contemplative dimension of the Gospel. We can't learn about Centering Prayer or any contemplative prayer practice by merely reading, thinking, or hearing about it. The only way we may really learn about Centering Prayer or silent contemplative prayer is to actually practice it daily over a period of time (say four to six weeks); then we may get an actual feel for it and realistically decide whether or not this kind of prayer is right for us at the present time. This is what we tell people at Introductory Centering Prayer Workshops.

In the last chapter, we tried to make it clear that Centering Prayer comes out of the Judeo–Christian tradition of "the Lord's Rest" or "resting in God." Given that *all* human beings are created in God's image and likeness (Gen. 1:26–27), and that "the light of the human race...which enlightens everyone" (John 1:4, 9) has been present in all humans from the beginning, it should not be surprising that the equivalent of "the Lord's Rest" and contemplative ways into it could have been discovered by sincere seekers of God and Truth in other times, places, and cultures. For example, Sanskrit is the sacred language of the ancient East Indian religions known to us in the West as

"Hinduism" and "Buddhism." The Sanskrit word for "meditation" is "*dhyana*"—which, translated into English, means "doing the wisdom." What greater wisdom could there be than practicing a prayer and following an inner meditative path that leads to conscious union with God? This is the common aim of mystics in all religions—a goal that transcends the *kataphatic* theological, doctrinal, and symbolic differences that distinguish and separate the various religions from one another as unique paths to God or Ultimate Reality.

Critics of Centering Prayer who mistakenly identify it with non-Christian religions may not know very much about Christian *apophatic* prayer, or about the deeper spiritual practices of those other religions. They appear to be creating false equivalencies by confusing surface similarities in the outer form or packaging of Centering Prayer mentioned earlier—e.g., outer similarities to TM or Zen, with the inner *kataphatic* contents of other religious faiths.

The superficial similarity of outer form does not in any way prove that there's a close similarity or identity of *kataphatic* theological content, faith, symbols, or religious belief. To draw such conclusions is to judge by appearances without looking into what's beneath them. We can't know for sure what's in a book by looking at its cover without actually opening and reading the book. Or, it's like assuming that if people in one religion kneel or bow down to God, then everyone who kneels or bows down to God must belong to that religion! We know this is not true. Everyone in every religion kneels or bows down to God, just as everyone in every religion prays and meditates to relate to God or the inner spiritual dimension of the soul. The outer similarity of religious form does not prove an inner identity of religious faith— that always depends on what's in the heart and mind of the one who prays and worships.

The simple fact that similarities in outer form across religious boundaries do not establish the presence of identity in *kataphatic* theological content is a key point that is generally missed by well-meaning critics of Centering Prayer who have doubts, objections, and concerns about Centering Prayer as a legitimate Christian spiritual practice.

As stated earlier, Centering Prayer is a relationship with Christ and a discipline of daily practice to foster the deepening and growth of that relationship. The theology of Centering Prayer is Christian and its conceptual background is based on traditional Christian spirituality combined with the discoveries of modern developmental and depth psychology, sociology, anthropology, physics, astronomy, and other sciences. These things have nothing to do with faith in the theology or metaphysics of Eastern religions or any other spiritual traditions. Centering Prayer's conceptual background comes out of the contemplative or mystical Judeo–Christian tradition,[5] and it includes the revelations of contemporary scientific research and discoveries. There are many important things known today about human nature and God's creation that were completely unknown to humans in ancient cultures and biblical times. The advances of science need to be integrated with the truths of religious faith, if religion is to remain truly relevant, up-to-date, and faithful to its sacred call.

≈

To clarify some additional misunderstandings about practicing the Centering Prayer method, Contemplative Outreach's brochure by Thomas Keating offers the following: "During this prayer we avoid analyzing our experience, harboring expectations, or aiming at some specific goal such as: Repeating the sacred word continuously; Having no thoughts; Making the mind a blank; Feeling peaceful or consoled; Achieving a spiritual experience." In Centering Prayer practice, we do not deliberately think about anything or try to make anything happen. We simply and humbly consent to and accept that *whatever* may be happening or not happening is God's Will for us in the present moment. This prayer works by God's grace and not by our efforts; and it works mostly *"in secret,"* in the unconscious, outside the sphere of our conscious awareness. It's an act of loving faith in which we simply trust that the divine action in our soul is doing whatever needs to be done to heal us spiritually and bring us closer in the divine relationship. Centering Prayer is very much a letting-go process wherein we "let go and let God," as they say in the twelve-step programs.

Some further clarifications regarding the Centering Prayer method to be found in Contemplative Outreach's brochure tell us:

> What Centering Prayer Is and Is Not: It is not a technique but a way of cultivating a deeper relationship with God; It is not a relaxation exercise but it may be quite refreshing; It is not a form of self-hypnosis but a way to quiet the mind while maintaining its alertness; It is not a charismatic gift but a path of transformation; It is not a parapsychological experience but an exercise of faith, hope and selfless love; It is not limited to the "felt" presence of God but is rather a deepening of faith in God's abiding presence; It is not reflective or spontaneous prayer, but simply resting in God beyond thoughts, words, and emotions.

These and the above are all very important points to be aware of for rightly understanding and practicing the method of Centering Prayer. In practicing Centering Prayer we do not try to suppress thoughts or to "make the mind a blank," as some poorly informed critics have assumed and stated. Either of these efforts would be counterproductive because entertaining the very idea of them involves us in more thinking and attachment to thoughts. As Thomas Keating has said, "it's not the absence of thoughts but *detachment from all* thoughts that indicates progress in practicing the Centering Prayer method." It's not humanly possible for us to stop our thoughts and the activities of our faculties of memory, intellect, emotions, and imagination. Only the divine action working in us can do that!

RECEPTIVITY

An important distinction Thomas Keating has pointed out regarding spiritual practices concerns the difference between concentrative practices and receptive ones. Concentrative practices depend on what we do and are primarily *kataphatic* (with images); since the practitioner or worshipper is focusing or concentrating on some particular thing or combination of things, e.g., a religious text, liturgy, symbol, ideal, energy center, or concept. *Kataphatic* religious practices define our religious identity as Christians or non-Christians and may also serve to prepare us for the deeper, more receptive *apophatic* practices in the mode of Matthew 6:6 and "resting in God." In contrast to concentrative practices, receptive practices depend primarily on what God does in us. Centering Prayer is a very receptive spiritual practice that complements our various *kataphatic* prayer practices; and that is intended to prepare our faculties (memory, intellect, and imagination) and our consciousness to directly receive the intuitive gift of God's presence and action within us.

In *kataphatic* prayer practices, we make use of our faculties as means of approaching and relating to God: concentrating on certain words, images, sounds, movements, ideals, etc. In receptive Centering Prayer, we let go of and detach from our faculties in order to simply consent to God's presence and action within us on the level of being without any specific preconceptions. This receptive consent or the intention of consenting to the divine presence and action of the Father, Son, and Holy Spirit within us distinguishes Centering Prayer from a variety of other practices that may lead one into the gift of contemplation. We do not try to "block out" our faculties by focusing attention on anything in particular to the exclusion of all else—which is what *kataphatic* concentrative practices often tend to do.

Instead, we simply allow whatever is in our consciousness to be there, to come and to go "like boats floating down a river," and we take a neutral, detached attitude toward the contents of our consciousness as much as we can; not by thinking about them but by "letting them all go by." Thomas Keating has noted that once something appears in our stream of consciousness, it's already on its way out as it "floats downstream." Whenever we realize we've become "engaged with our thoughts," we simply return to our sacred word or other symbol (e.g., the sacred breath or gaze) to renew our intention of consenting to God's presence and action within us. It's as simple as that. It only requires our humble patience and persistence, and willingness to consent to and allow whatever the divine action is doing in us.

Centering Prayer works automatically in the unconscious, to the degree that we are actually consenting. So, regardless of what our conscious contents may be in Centering Prayer, the inner work of the Spirit is happening and moving forward in us *"in secret"* (Matt. 6:6), as we humbly and receptively trust and consent to God's hidden activity in us. Hence, Centering Prayer is very much an act of faith that gradually moves us deeper and deeper into the intimacy of the divine relationship—where God reveals more and more of the truth of our soul to us. Without faith and trust on our part, this cannot happen. Via the receptivity and consent of Centering Prayer, we are surrendering control of the prayer and placing the power of its direction and action into God's Hands.

The conscious, explicit intention of consenting to the inner movements of the Spirit in our soul (which are mostly unseen), is a distinguishing characteristic of Centering Prayer that sets it apart from a variety of other spiritual practices and prayer forms. In contrast, *kataphatic* devotional and concentrative practices implicitly consent to God's Will while focusing on their objects of prayer or meditation—e.g., the Rosary, Blessed Sacrament, Sacred Heart of Jesus, a Scripture passage, or Stations of the Cross for Christians; and mantras, visualizations, energy currents and centers (*chakras*) in the physical or subtle body for non-Christians. Some of these *kataphatic* practices are precise techniques that need to be done in a particular way to produce a correspondingly particular result. Centering Prayer, on the other hand, is not a precise technique but a more general method defined by its four basic guidelines (see above). The "results" of Centering Prayer may be anything ranging from deep rest in God to full blown unloading of the unconscious (see below). What happens in Centering Prayer does not depend on what we do, but on what the divine action does in us. It's all about our consent.

We may not relax the mind into pure receptivity until it's in relative peace; that is, peace with our conscience and freedom from afflictive emotions and inner turmoil. Some religious devotions and concentrative techniques are designed to bring the mind to peace, so that it may then go deeper into nonconceptual meditation or resting in God. Other *kataphatic* prayers and meditations are designed to activate particular forces or energies in the soul, to transform the practitioner's personality and consciousness. Centering Prayer leaves all of this to the divine action's work in the soul, which may, at times, temporarily quiet our faculties and draw us into the Lord's Rest. Centering Prayer's explicit intention to consent and leave the results to God distinguishes it from all of these other kinds of practices, whether they're Christian or non-Christian. Ultimately, all differences are *kataphatic*. In the purely *apophatic* there are no differences, because, in that non-created realm of silence and rest, we're beyond thoughts, words, images, emotions, memories, and concepts. Hence, the *apophatic* dimension of silent contemplation may serve as a fertile ground for Christian unity and harmony among religions.

≈

Misunderstanding of Centering Prayer is liable to arise when individuals who are unaware of the distinctions between the *kataphatic* and the *apophatic*, and between concentrative techniques and receptive methods such as Centering Prayer, unknowingly confuse Centering Prayer with various concentrative practices. This is especially true when the container or surface outer appearance of receptive Centering Prayer and concentrative practices look alike from the outside—as in the above examples of Transcendental Meditation and Zen Meditation, or in the cases of Mindfulness Meditation and other "witnessing" practices of self-observation. In such concentrative practices, the practitioner inwardly concentrates on or repeats a mantra throughout the meditation (as in the initial stages of TM); thinks about a *koan* or paradoxical riddle (as in some forms of Zen Meditation); watches bodily activities like the breath; observes or concentrates the faculties of memory, intellect, emotions, or imagination. In Centering Prayer practice, one concentrates deliberately on none of these things but inwardly disregards all of them, simply letting them go by while quietly consenting to the divine presence and action within.

Though outwardly it may appear to be similar to a variety of Christian and non-Christian concentrative practices, inwardly Centering Prayer is quite distinct and different from all of them. Centering Prayer's "alert receptivity" and inward consent to the divine presence and action deep in the soul is what sets it apart from other Christian and non-Christian prayer or meditative practices of a *kataphatic* and concentrative nature. As Basil Pennington has put it, the method, theology, and process of Centering Prayer are a modern crystallization of the ancient Christian Contemplative Tradition.[6]

HUMBLE PIE: REVEALING AND HEALING

Thanks to the discoveries of modern psychology; and to the pioneering work of Thomas Keating and others; it's now possible to understand the psychospiritual dynamics of the soul's spiritual transformation in the divine relationship better than ever before. Thomas Keating writes in *Intimacy with God* (p. 86), "Centering Prayer involves a good deal of interface with psychology; in fact, it was specifically developed as a dialogue between contemporary psychological models and the classical language of the Christian spiritual path...the prayer itself encourages the emergence of previously unconscious material." This is a key point regarding the process of Centering Prayer when done as a daily practice over an extended period of time. A person who commits to Centering Prayer as a path to deepening the divine relationship needs to be willing and prepared to face the positive and negative contents of her or his personal unconscious; and this includes the dark, rejected side of one's personality along with the toxic energies of whatever unhealed emotional wounds and afflictive emotions are harbored there—i.e., "what is hidden in darkness" (1 Cor. 4:5).

The process of Centering Prayer is all about purification, healing, and transformation in the soul as we work to grow closer to God in the divine relationship. Drawing from the incredible breakthrough insights of modern psychology, Thomas Keating came up with the descriptive term "unloading the unconscious," to indicate this inner spiritual process that is brought about by the divine action in us via our consenting to it in Centering Prayer. This same key process of inner healing and transformation is indicated by Paul in 1 Corinthians 4:5, where he tells us insightfully: "When the Lord comes he will bring to light what is hidden in darkness and will manifest the motives of our hearts." Let's take a brief look at this important passage from Paul in terms of the Four Senses of Scripture:

In the outer literal sense, the Lord's coming is interpreted as external and is envisioned as happening on a universal planetary or cosmic scale—e.g., at "the end of time," (cf. Matt. 25:31–33). This most radical world-changing event, called "the *parousia*," was apparently expected by many of the first Christians to be imminent; that is, that it would happen within their own lifetimes, (Luke 21:25–33; 1 Thes. 4:15–5:4). Similarly, the Second Coming of Jesus in the outer literal sense has been predicted and expected by Christians several times right up to the present day; but it obviously has not yet taken place on an outer planetary or universal cosmic scale. Jesus himself says the time of the world's ending and of the Lord's coming—when all shall be held accountable—is known only to the Father (Mark 13:32).

In modern times, Tielhard de Chardin, S.J., has interpreted the literal Second Coming of Christ as an evolutionary transformation of human consciousness into divine consciousness on a planetary scale.[7] This intriguing idea suggests that once a certain critical mass of human beings have evolved into conscious spiritual union and wholeness in the love of Christ, the collective influence of their goodwill, solidarity with all humanity, and harmony with God's Divine Will shall serve to awaken the spiritual presence of Divine Love in the hearts of all willing human beings on a collective planetary scale— then we'll all know and experience consciously our spiritual unity as members of the Body of Christ in the heart of Divine Love. According to de Chardin's idea (which is based on a synthesis of Christian biblical spirituality and modern scientific discoveries), each human being who grows spiritually closer to God in the divine relationship is helping to bring about the Second Coming of our Lord, Jesus Christ. The inner transformation process of Centering Prayer has much to contribute to bringing Christ into the world of human consciousness and relationships in this way.

In the moral sense of Scripture (which may be interpreted both outwardly and inwardly), the Lord's coming, "bringing to light what's hidden in darkness" (i.e., into consciousness what is hidden in the unconscious), and "manifesting the motives of our hearts," reveals the full truth of each soul, revealing our true self as spiritual beings, exposing all lies and falsity, and manifesting the righteousness of truth and justice for all to see. When the light of God's truth shines in us and throughout created reality, both *within and among us,* there shall be no dark hiding places left for denials, cover-ups, or false, evil entities of the hidden shadows. We are each responsible and accountable for all that we create and manifest. Thankfully, our Christian God of Love is the God of forgiveness, mercy, and compassion, as we may clearly see in the teachings, life, death, and resurrection of Jesus. The moral sense of Christ's coming may be experienced individually in each of us as we evolve through the inner process of our individual spiritual journey; and ultimately it will be experienced by everyone, either following physical death or, for all of those still living as humans on Earth, in the great collective transformational transition of the Lord's coming or *parousia* at the end of time.

In the inner allegorical sense of Scripture, the Lord's coming is the manifestation of the divine action in each individual soul. This is inevitable for all of us, whether it takes place in our present lifetime or in the next life after the spiritual transition of our physical death. The inner process of Centering Prayer and its unloading of the unconscious are about consenting to and hastening this process so that we may go through some or all of it and be of better service to God in this present lifetime. When Jesus tells us: "The truth shall set you Free" (John 8:32), he is talking about the truth of our soul. When the Lord manifests in us to reveal what's hidden in our personal darkness, and to show us our secret motives, he does this to bring us to reality and to free us from the inner obstacles that are preventing us from growing further into the love of Christ in the divine relationship.

The purpose of the unloading process, which challenges our faith and trust in God, and which can be quite disturbing, frightening, and humiliating, is to heal and transform us into a *"new creation"* in Christ according to God's plan for us. This, ultimately, is the whole point and purpose of the process of Centering Prayer. In the inner spiritual sense of Scripture, the Lord's coming is simply our full and intimate communion and union with God in Divine Love through the gift of *apophatic* contemplation and the Lord's Rest. We go through the soul's dark nights of uncertainty, doubt, and dread, and through the unloading of the unconscious, in order to be healed and transformed into who God created us to become. It's through this process—which is allegorically modeled for us in the life of Jesus, especially in the Paschal Mystery—that we are able to grow up into and receive the fullness of our divine inheritance as souls created in God's (Love's) image and likeness.[8]

Though we all possess the same marvelous divine potential, what our negative unconscious contents "hidden in darkness" actually are is different for each of us. Invariably, they're related to each person's unique complex of unhealed wounds, afflictive emotions, and the irrational emotional happiness programs we've unconsciously created to compensate for those wounds (see chapter 1 for details regarding this). We all have our own individual history, strengths, weaknesses, unresolved issues, and personal "demons" hidden within us—whatever they may be. The emergence of this material into consciousness is what Thomas Keating has called "the unloading of the unconscious." When the unconscious unloads, our unhealed past comes alive for us in the present, exactly as it was when originally experienced and repressed. This can be quite disturbing and confusing; especially if one has no conceptual background regarding the unloading of the unconscious and its essential role in spiritual healing, growth, and integrating or transforming the split-off parts of the soul.

For most people, the unloading process doesn't really begin until after they've been practicing Centering Prayer for a couple of years or so—and they're prepared to experience it. In some cases, however, unloading begins rather quickly and an individual may not be prepared to experience it. The timing and contents of unloading depend on the individual psychodynamics of what's just beneath the surface consciousness when a person begins practicing Centering Prayer; and they depend on the action of God's grace in the soul. The dynamic of human free will is always in play, as well as the dynamic of *how* we relate to God in the divine relationship. Successfully negotiating the unloading process requires a deep level of trust and faith in the divine action, and it requires tolerance for uncertainty in the dynamics of our deepening relationship with God. "Without trust there can be no relationship," and without trust there can be no "letting go and letting God" be God in us.

So, how and when the unconscious unloads is different for different people, as are the specific unconscious contents and issues with which each individual will sooner or later be confronted; if he or she is serious about the spiritual journey and persists in daily Centering Prayer practice long enough. A "transformative spirituality" like Centering Prayer is markedly different from a "feel good" spirituality that engages the physical senses and the faculties of memory, intellect, emotion, and imagination while avoiding "what's hidden in darkness." Unloading the unconscious is an essential part of the work the Holy Spirit does in our soul to remove our inner obstacles, prepare us for deeper contemplation, and bring us closer in the divine relationship. Without the healing and transformative action of this inner work, we would simply remain stuck in preliminary stages of the spiritual journey; repeating the patterns of our current status quo in the divine relationship, with our hidden unconscious obstacles remaining fixed in place and keeping us unable to evolve forward.

This process of cleaning out or "evacuating the unconscious" is generally not pleasant. Traditionally it's been called "the purification process." In this process, everything in us that's opposed to the Gospel and to the love of Christ is gradually eliminated from the soul, either by destruction, by expulsion, or by transformation. Allegorically, this inner purifying work of the Spirit in us corresponds to the Baptism of John; that is the cleansing baptism of water and repentance by which we "change the direction in which we're looking for happiness"—i.e., we outgrow our childish emotional programs for happiness. This crucial and fundamental change may not occur in us without significant changes taking place in the unconscious roots of our motivation and desire nature—which need to be brought into harmony and alignment with "the mind of Christ." The consent of Centering Prayer takes us directly into this process, since by it we willingly give the Holy Spirit permission to do God's work in our soul.

In his excellent book, *Contemplative Prayer*, Thomas Merton quotes Peter of Celles, a twelfth century contemplative Benedictine monk:

> God works in us while we rest in him. Beyond all grasping is this work of the Creator, itself creative, this rest. For such work exceeds all rest, in its tranquility. This rest, in its effect, shines forth as more productive than any work. Therefore let this action or rest of our contemplation be fashioned so as to reproduce, even though only in faint or sketchy lines, one model [of work and rest which is in God]. (p. 59).

This work of God in our soul is our redemption in Christ. It only requires our *yes*—our consent to the process and willingness to faithfully put up with its ups and downs as we patiently persist in our daily Centering Prayer or other receptive contemplative practice.

Not everyone is ready or willing to face the truth of their soul through the unloading of the unconscious, especially individuals who've never heard of such a thing. When the unconscious starts unloading its toxic contents (e.g., the emotional wounds of unhealed memories, broken relationships, unresolved conflicts, and afflictive emotions), it always feels like you're getting worse. Unless a person is aware of the unloading process and its immense value for spiritual growth, the natural human inclination is to do whatever one can to avoid this—and it's not unusual for such unsettling experiences to seem like and be misinterpreted as attacks from inner or outer evil spirits or demons, especially if one is thinking of such things.

When we have contact with disowned and rejected parts of our soul that we're in denial about (i.e., its shadow contents), these are typically experienced as alien outside entities and not part of who we are. In modern depth psychology (e.g., Jungian Psychology) this externalization of unwanted unconscious contents in the soul has been called "projection." It's an "ego-defense mechanism" and way of denying responsibility for what we don't like or may fear in our self. This psychological denial process and panic in the face of unwanted unconscious contents has led to some serious misunderstandings about Centering Prayer and its potential value for good in the soul. In the early 1990s, some strong criticisms and objections to Centering Prayer across the theological divide arose as the result of a few uninformed individuals apparently experiencing premature unloading, being frightened, and then having extreme misgivings about the safety of Centering Prayer and what it may open us up to.

Without a sound conceptual background regarding the inner purification, healing, and transformation process (including unloading the unconscious), an uninformed person experiencing unloading is liable to become distrustful, frightened, and to have serious doubts about the safety and value of Centering Prayer as a healthy spiritual practice. This is why having a good and realistic conceptual background regarding the process of Centering Prayer is so important. Without it, one is literally operating in the dark and liable to fall prey to all kinds of negative thoughts, doubts, imaginings, fears, and delusions— once the unloading process begins in earnest. Though relatively rare, there have been instances where unprepared individuals have reacted with panic and paranoia to their unloading processes, and this has led to some unfortunate misunderstandings of and prejudices against Centering Prayer; even to the point where Centering Prayer has been falsely branded as an evil New-Age practice that opens you up to dangerous forces of darkness and to Satan himself.[9]

Centering Prayer is not dangerous for most people; but it's not the right prayer practice for everyone either. Centering Prayer is appropriate for people who are in reasonably good mental health, who seek a deeper, more intimate relationship with God, and who feel attracted or called to praying in silence. The receptivity of Centering Prayer opens us directly to the energies of the unconscious—which, as explained above, can be challenging. So it's important that people who practice Centering Prayer are relatively well grounded and comfortable in their human identity with sufficient mental stability and ego strength to face, accept, and integrate the truth of their soul (including its dark side) as the divine action may reveal it to them. People need to know what they're getting into when they take up and commit themselves to daily Centering Prayer practice. What comes up depends on what's inside us, and this is different for each of us. Having a good conceptual background including foreknowledge about the unloading process allows us to recognize and even "welcome" the unloading process when it happens. It always means that God is "getting down to business" with us when unloading begins; that is, the business of our purification, healing, and transformation.

Fortunately, most individuals for whom Centering Prayer may not be appropriate are not drawn to or interested in this or any other receptive prayer practice. Perhaps they sense intuitively that they're not yet ready to face what's buried in their unconscious, and that Centering Prayer could open them up to this prematurely. For such individuals, concentrative prayer practices, where they're more consciously in control of the praying process, are more appropriate. In concentrative practices, one works with the unconscious indirectly, through the agencies of the faculties (memory, intellect, emotions, and imagination), using *kataphatic* images, sounds, movements, concepts, etc. to communicate with the unconscious and thereby act upon its various energies and contents. As we "speak" to our unconscious, with thoughts, images, and the intentions of our heart, it responds to us correspondingly by its own law.

As mentioned earlier, Centering Prayer is a deepening of our relationship with Christ into the commitment levels of friendship and full intimacy or union of life. In the process of Centering Prayer, God plays the active role and we rest in the receptive role. In the intimacy of the divine relationship and our daily Centering Prayer practice, God reveals us to our self. This inevitably includes both our positive potentials and humiliating self-knowledge of the dark side of our personality. There's typically a back-and-forth alternation between affirmation and humiliation, or between "consolation and desolation." If we're not prepared to accept all of this, and if we're unwilling to "own" our dark side and take responsibility for the full truth of our soul, then we'll resist any challenging or shattering of our ego's homemade self-image, and we may resort to ego-defense mechanisms like denial and projection—so that our unloaded unconscious contents will be perceived as not ours but alien and separate like an "evil spirit" or "attacking demon."

This is not intended to deny the real existence of evil entities and demonic influences in the invisible psychospiritual realms. However, such malefic forces are spiritually attracted and may form bonds *only* with other beings whose conscious or unconscious spiritual attitudes and desires are in sympathy with their own. For this reason, most anyone who sincerely prays and seeks closeness and harmony with God in the love of Christ will be under the protection of the Holy Spirit and would not be a "spiritual magnet" for evil entities. Hence, even when toxic unconscious contents that come up in the unloading process are experienced as foreign external entities, the chances of this being objectively true are very remote; especially if we consider the facts that what we've denied in our self we have "cast out" and alienated from our consciousness (so naturally our consciousness will experience it as separate or "external"); and whatever lives in us belongs to us, whether we've created it or not.[10] Centering Prayer is a practical means to deepening our relationship with Christ and is part of the Christian Contemplative Heritage. It is not in any way connected to "evil entities" or "dark forces," as some uninformed critics of Centering Prayer have wrongly assumed and alleged.

It's a simple fact that unconscious contents in the soul are changed whenever they become conscious. How they change depends on how we respond or react to them. If we understand that unloading the unconscious is an essential and necessary aspect of the inner purification and healing process initiated by the divine action in us via the consent of Centering Prayer, then we may be able to trust the process enough to accept and even welcome negative unconscious contents that come up for us. This acceptance of them will change them for the better. On the other hand, if we don't understand about the unloading process and are shocked, disturbed, or frightened by afflictive emotions and other negative unconscious contents that come up, then we'll be inclined to deny, reject, and want to get rid of them by running away or repressing them back down into the unconscious—if we can. This will change them for the worse.

When we reject wounded parts of our soul and the memories attached to them, they become negative unconscious contents that function destructively against us, expressing an adversarial attitude toward our conscious attitudes and intentions. Hence, they become our psychospiritual shadow or the dark side of our personality.[11] It may well be that, as these wounded and rejected parts of our soul oppose and create problems in us, they do this to get our attention and are really crying out in pain for recognition, help, and healing.

Centering Prayer does not create these negative unconscious contents; we do, in response to experiences we cannot face or accept, especially in early life when we feel helpless and overwhelmed. It's through the unloading process of Centering Prayer that our negative unconscious contents may be revealed to us, as part of the divine therapy that aims to heal the broken divide in our soul. The answer to this problem of how the inner conflict with our shadow may be healed is by gradually accepting and integrating it into our consciousness and personality—which requires recognizing that it's actually a wounded part of our soul, and then humbly accepting it as it is (similar to how

God loves and accepts us just as we are). This healing recognition of acceptance and love transforms our shadow and eventually converts it into a valuable ally.

≈

Unloading the unconscious (the purification process) takes us from the beginning stages of our spiritual journey in the divine relationship into and through the intermediate stages. Unloading helps us to know our self, the truth of our soul, as God knows us and loves us. It's important to appreciate the fact that different individuals experience unloading in different ways at different times. Sometimes it's dramatic and intense (as, for example, when a lot of pent-up anger or sadness surfaces); and at other times unloading may be subtle and barely noticeable. Anytime we overreact or over-compensate to people or events in daily life, unloading is likely to be involved. Each individual's unique unloading process depends on such things as: what's inside that particular soul; the individual's temperament; life history and current situation; where one is in the divine relationship (i.e., on the level of acquaintanceship, friendliness, friendship, or full intimacy and union of life); our level of consent to the divine action; and how the Holy Spirit chooses to work with us. Hence, we can't predict what the unloading process will be for anyone, including our self. The spiritual journey is an adventure that's full of surprises; and, in the end, they will all be wonderful surprises we couldn't have imagined!

THE DANCE THAT HAS NO WEAVER

To summarize: Centering Prayer is a relationship with Christ and a discipline to foster the deepening and growth of that relationship. It prepares us for the gift of silent contemplation that corresponds to the spiritual sense of Scripture. Centering Prayer is a modern synthesis of the Christian Contemplative Tradition, which has its roots in the Old Testament tradition of "the Lord's Rest" or "Sabbath Rest," and in the allegorical interpretation of Jesus' wisdom saying in Matthew

6:6, "When you pray, go into your inner room, close the door, and pray to your Father in secret; and your Father who sees in secret will repay you."

Centering Prayer is not a precise technique that produces particular results when done properly. It is, rather, a receptive, open-ended, "hands-on" method that may be learned and understood only by doing it regularly over an extended period of time. The essence of Centering Prayer is consenting or intending to consent to Christ's presence and action in us and in our life. This consenting includes willingness to let go of personal desires or agendas (happiness programs) that are not in harmony with the Gospel values of love, truth, freedom, and forgiveness for all.

Consenting to the divine presence and action calls for a certain pliability to follow the inner urgings of the Holy Spirit, and willingness to see the full truth of our soul as God may reveal it to us through the process of Centering Prayer: that is, in the divine therapy and unloading of the unconscious (which goes on in daily life as well as during our prayer time, and which is different for each of us). Our growth in the two types of self-knowledge (humiliating and affirming) brings our human consciousness into increasing intimacy with God's Consciousness in the divine relationship. We need to trust the divine action enough to be willing to slow down, relax, let go, and die to our homemade human false self (our sense of personal identity apart from our life in God).

As human beings we have the capacity to relate to God both outwardly and inwardly. Our full exercise of this capacity through a variety of ways of praying (relating to God) crosses and reconciles the theological divide separating our perceptions of God as external to us versus God within us and us within God (the Western and Scriptural Models). Our different possible ways of relating to God are outlined in the model of the Four Levels of Relationship discussed in chapter 3: acquaintanceship, friendliness, friendship, and full intimacy or union of life. The various ways of prayer, or ways of relating to God (or another person), are also expressed in the Four Senses of Scripture (literal, moral, allegorical, and spiritual); in *Lectio Divina*; and in the process of Centering Prayer.

God takes the initiative by inviting us into a deeper, more intimate relationship; so that we may eventually come to live all of our daily life consciously in relation to God, and in response to the urging and guidance of the Holy Spirit within us. We are always free to say *yes* or *no* to God's loving invitation. We're always free to open or close our mind and heart to God's subtle voice within us (our conscience). The invitation comes from God's side of the divine relationship we've had with God since our creation as an individual soul in God; and the choice is always ours. The bottom line of the divine invitation is that God wants us to know God loves us and is within us. Our aim in the service of Centering Prayer and Contemplative Outreach is to do whatever we can to help people grow closer to God in the two-way divine relationship. This is our bottom line in service to the divine plan or intention of our loving God.

A life of prayer is a life lived in relation to God. The purpose of Centering Prayer is to say *yes* to God's invitation, and to deepen this relationship by consenting and ultimately wedding our soul's will to God's most loving and righteous Will for us and others. In our faith relationship, we trust and know that *whatever* God wills for us is what is presently and eternally best for us as seekers of love, truth, and freedom in the spiritual journey. This is what we are about in consenting to God's presence and action through our daily Centering Prayer practice.

There appear to be three general critical objections to Centering Prayer that come from misinformation and misunderstanding about the prayer. These three critical challenges to Centering Prayer are: 1) doubting that Centering Prayer is a legitimate Christian prayer; 2) claims that Centering Prayer is dangerous and liable to open us up to "evil" influences; and 3) some criticisms and objections claim that Centering Prayer and its conceptual background are contrary to the teaching and doctors of the Catholic Church. The first two of these common misunderstandings and objections to Centering Prayer have been addressed in this and the previous chapter; and the third one has been touched upon. A fourth category of critical objections is aimed at the teachings of Thomas Keating and Contemplative Outreach.

So far in this book, we've introduced some core elements of Centering Prayer's conceptual background; we've discussed the theological divide and the divine relationship that resolves it; we've explained the origins of Centering Prayer within the context of the Christian Contemplative Tradition; and, in discussing the unloading of the unconscious, we've explained that, though not appropriate for everyone, Centering Prayer is not dangerous for those who are properly prepared with the appropriate conceptual background. As mentioned earlier, Centering Prayer may be appropriate for sincere individuals who are in reasonably good mental health, who desire a deeper, more intimate relationship with God, and who feel attracted or called to praying quietly in receptive silence (in addition to their other ways of praying). The only practical way to find out if Centering Prayer is right for you is to try it daily for a month or two and then decide. Studying Thomas Keating's *Open Mind, Open Heart,* participating in a regular prayer group, and talking with people who are already grounded in Centering Prayer will also be helpful. It's assumed that one is living a life based on Christian Gospel values.

In the following chapters, we'll continue discussing the theological divide and divine relationship by looking further into objections to Centering Prayer, and we'll address some misinterpretations of Thomas Keating's teaching that challenge the legitimacy of Centering Prayer and its conceptual background. As we proceed, may we abide patiently in humility, peace, and preciousness in the Lord's merciful presence, recalling the prayerful words of Saint Augustine: "Our hearts are forever restless, Lord, until they rest in Thee."

6

AFFIRMING AND OPPOSING CENTERING PRAYER

PRAYER OF CONSENT

Centering Prayer is much more a prayer of receptive "intention" than it is a prayer of active "attention." Intention is an act of our will whereas attention is a focusing of our mind or consciousness. As mentioned earlier, it's Centering Prayer's intention to consent to God's presence and action in us that differentiates it from other, more concentrative types of prayer and meditation. *Explicitly* consenting or having the intention of consenting to God's presence and action in us is the heart and soul of Centering Prayer. Both intention and attention are internal acts or dispositions of the soul that may not be seen or detected on the outer, surface level of physical observation—which is comparable to the literal sense of Scripture. Hence, outwardly, two or more individuals sitting in quiet prayer or meditation may appear to be doing the same thing; yet inwardly, they may be doing very different things—e.g., concentrating with one or more of the soul's faculties (memory, intellect, emotions, and imagination), versus openly resting in "the space between thoughts"; or observing one's physical and non-physical activities versus detaching or letting go of thoughts (which may still be present) and consenting to God's presence and action within. These distinctions are very important.

Critics who compare Centering Prayer to a variety of outwardly similar spiritual practices, and who conclude that what they're doing must be the same, are apparently unaware of the vital inner distinctions regarding what individuals are actually doing or not doing *internally* in prayer and meditation practices—which may be concentrative or receptive, *kataphatic* or *apophatic*. Outer similarities are no guarantee of inner identities; and the potential differences may go far deeper than this, if we consider the variety of religious, theological, motivational, and conceptual contexts in which individuals may enter into and engage their spiritual practices. To point out the difference between "intention" and "attention," Thomas Keating has described Centering Prayer as being primarily about "heartfulness," as compared to "mindfulness," which is characteristic of a number of other quite different practices that may outwardly appear to be the same or similar.[1]

In Centering Prayer, intention concerns our will toward God; that is, our will to consent to God's Will for us. If our intention to consent to the divine presence and action in us were pure and unadulterated, then we'd already be in conscious divine union from our side of the divine relationship—just as God is already in full conscious union with each of us from God's side of the relationship. The inevitable implication of this, of our needing to consciously intend to consent to God's presence and action, is that there are parts of us that are opposed to consenting to God's Will for us. In other words, we're not yet free to fully consent to the divine presence and action in us. There's something fearful in us (i.e., our human persona or false self) that resists and may not trust God's Will or plan for us; and we may be very reluctant to consciously admit this unwelcome fact to our self, since it likely contradicts the fragile positive image we may hold of our self as a religious person or spiritual seeker. No need to worry though, God knows absolutely *everything* about us, understands our position, loves us exactly as we are, and invites us into the divine relationship.

The doubt-filled parts of our self that are opposed to consenting to the divine presence and action are rooted in the childish self-centeredness of our unhealed emotional wounds, afflictive emotions, and the unhealthy happiness programs we've unconsciously created as distorted compensations and overreactions to the pain of those wounds (as described in chapter 1). We can't get directly at the source of our inner obstacles and resistance to God's Will because it's unconscious or "*hidden in darkness*" where we can't see it. Fortunately, however, the merciful and compassionate divine presence and action in us does see it. This is a fundamental premise of the divine therapy and Centering Prayer's conceptual background.

God respects the integrity of our free will, and it's our sincere intention of consenting to the divine presence and action in us that gives the Holy Spirit permission to do something about the self-defeating, life-negating inner obstacles and resistance of our unhealthy motivations—so that we may freely grow closer to God from our side of the divine relationship. This is the secret of the inner process of Centering Prayer that may not be observed from the outside by critics or by anyone else. It's deeply intimate and personal between the individual who prayerfully consents and God, who does the healing and work of transformation in the soul.

Judging Centering Prayer by its outer form or appearance is similar to judging a book by its cover, title, and appearance without reading the book and finding out what's really inside it. Such superficial "judgments" may give rise to "false equivalencies" and are more guesswork or speculation than factual study or actual experimentation. If someone does try to practice Centering Prayer without an understanding of its conceptual background, then he or she is unprepared, "operating in the dark," and may jump to faulty conclusions when the unconscious starts to unload, as explained in the last chapter. Our consent in Centering Prayer initiates an inner dynamic of purification, healing, and transformation carried out by the Holy Spirit in our soul. We need to be prepared for this. When we're prepared, Centering Prayer is perfectly safe for most people; and our commitment to daily Centering Prayer practice is a commitment to the divine relationship in faith and trust on the level of friendship (see chapter 3).

Sincerely consenting to God's presence and action in Centering Prayer fulfills the moral sense of Scripture on the deepest level. The moral sense of God's Word emanates from our innate spiritual conscience (if we can "hear" it), and tells us to be truthful and loving in all our relations with self, others, God, and God's Creation. Being truthful and loving is the universal basis of God's (Love's) Cosmic

Spiritual Law that governs the moral/ethical integrity of evolving souls, consciousness, and created reality. Our consenting to God's presence and action is a spiritual commitment to see and accept the truth of our soul in *all* of its aspects as God may choose to reveal it to us. This is our "Yes" to God in deepening the divine relationship.

Each deepening level of consent to God's presence and action in us requires a deeper level of trust and willingness to be vulnerable to see the truth of our soul. Early-life and later-life wounding, betrayal, loss, and abandonment all negatively impact our ability to trust other people, God, and our own unconscious. We never know what may be hidden *"in darkness"* inside us. This is why "letting go and letting God" can be so difficult; and it's also why allowing God to heal our emotional wounds is so essential for our soul's growth into the divine relationship.

As long as our emotional wounds remain unhealed and buried in the unconscious, our fearful inner resistance to growing closer to God in the divine relationship will also remain intact—even when our conscious attitude and desire is to grow closer to God. This is the basic crisis of each person's challenge in the spiritual journey; and it's only the divine action in us that may free us from the stagnant impasse of our unconscious inner obstacles and resistances. Hence, the consent of Centering Prayer is needed to allow Christ to be God in us and to redeem our soul from the sticky unconscious mire in which it's stuck. Until we're ready and willing to really let go and consent to God's Will, our tendency will be to keep God at a distance from our side of the divine relationship; that is, we'll tend to relate to our most intimate God Who loves us completely on the levels of acquaintanceship, friendliness, or preliminary friendship.

Consenting to God's presence and action is the fundamental principle of Centering Prayer. This consenting translates into our saying "Yes" to God's Will for us; and it becomes our inner allegorical participation in the Paschal Mystery of Christ and the Way of the Cross; for in consenting to God's presence and action we are agreeing to *whatever* God needs to do in us to bring us into the Love of Christ.

This inevitably includes trusting our divine therapist throughout the sometimes painful or disturbing unloading and purification of our unconscious.

I have yet to see a criticism of Centering Prayer that openly and accurately acknowledges that consenting to God's presence and action in us is the practical basis of this humble prayer. Hence, Centering Prayer is typically (and probably unknowingly) misrepresented by those who oppose it. Consenting, and ultimately surrendering our self to God's loving Will for us is what Centering Prayer—as taught by Thomas Keating and Contemplative Outreach—is all about. It's a healing process of renewal and rebirth in Christ that gradually works its way from our soul's outermost periphery into its inmost true center—and, as Thomas Merton suggests—through that center we may pass into the Ultimate Mystery and Reality of God, which we may call "Divine Love!" Centering Prayer calls for a serious, faithful commitment to the divine relationship; and Centering Prayer's faithful daily practice prepares us for the precious spiritual gift of what the *Catechism of the Catholic Church* calls "contemplative prayer" (see below).

THE CATHOLIC CATECHISM AND CENTERING PRAYER

Since consenting to God's presence and action in us "is the heart and soul of Centering Prayer," the essential effect of Centering Prayer's explicit intention is to gradually unite our personal will to God's Will for us—*whatever* that may be. This is a faith relationship based in trust and longing for intimacy with God. "We do not know how to pray as we ought" (Rom. 8:26), so we ask the Holy Spirit's divine action to pray in us for us. This is the inner essence of Centering Prayer—which is completely in harmony with the Christian Scriptures ("*Thy Will be done*"), and with the teaching of the Catholic Church (see below). To anyone who thinks or who has been told that Centering Prayer "is contrary to our Catholic faith," I invite you to do some thoughtful reading in the *Catechism of the Catholic Church,* specifically in the beautiful section on "Contemplative Prayer" (pp. 650–652, para. 2,709–2,719). This discussion includes implicit references to both *kataphatic* and *apophatic* contemplation. Here are some pertinent excerpts from the *Catechism* with some commentary from me:

> Entering contemplative prayer is like entering into the Eucharistic liturgy: we "gather up" the heart, recollect our whole being under the prompting of the Holy Spirit, abide in the dwelling place of the Lord which we are, awaken our faith in order to enter into the presence of him who awaits us. We let our masks fall and turn our hearts back to the Lord who loves us, so as to hand ourselves over to him as an offering to be purified and transformed. (para. 2,711)

This beautiful passage captures the essence and trusting vulnerability of the Centering Process, which prepares and takes us through *acquired contemplation* (what we may do in practicing Centering Prayer) into the gift of *infused contemplation* (what God does in us).

"...for everything is grace from God. Contemplative prayer is the poor and humble surrender to the loving will of the Father in ever deeper union with his beloved Son" (para. 2,712). As Thomas Keating teaches, "Consent leads to surrender."

"Contemplative prayer...is a gift, a grace; it can be accepted only in humility and poverty. Contemplative prayer is a covenant relationship established by God within our hearts.... [It is] a communion in which the Holy Trinity conforms man [and woman], the image of God, 'to his likeness'" (para. 2,713). The consent of Centering Prayer begins and sustains this process.

"Contemplative prayer is the preeminently intense time of prayer. In it the Father strengthens our inner being with power through his Spirit 'that Christ may dwell in [our] hearts through faith' and we may be 'grounded in love'" (para. 2,714).

"Contemplative prayer is hearing the Word of God. Far from being passive, such attentiveness is the obedience of faith, the unconditional acceptance of a servant, and the loving commitment of a child. It participates in the 'Yes' of the Son become servant and the Fiat of God's lowly handmaid [Mary's "Yes" to God's request to bear his Son]" (para. 2,716). This is precisely what's meant allegorically in Centering Prayer by consenting to God's presence and action in us, so that our soul's individual will may ultimately be wed to "the mind of Christ" and to God's Will for us.

"Contemplative prayer is silence, the 'symbol of the world to come' or 'silent love.' Words in this kind of prayer are not speeches; they are like kindling that feeds the fire of love. In this silence, unbearable to the 'outer' man [false self], the Father speaks to us his incarnate Word, who suffered, died, and rose; in this silence the Spirit of adoption enables us to share in the prayer of Jesus" (para. 2,717).

"Contemplative prayer is a union with the prayer of Christ insofar as it makes us participate in his mystery. The mystery of Christ is celebrated by the Church in the Eucharist, and the Holy Spirit makes it come alive in contemplative prayer so that our charity will manifest it in our acts" (para. 2,718). The movement from contemplation to action suggested here is extremely important. We're to become instruments for the Holy Spirit in this world, co-creators with God in service and implementation of the divine plan for Creation's perfection—as the Spirit leads us and inspires us via the intuitive gift of contemplation.

The counter movement from action to contemplation is equally important. We see this modeled in the life and ministry of Jesus in the Gospels, with his periods of withdrawal from active ministry into solitude—to commune with the Father, receive inner guidance, and recharge his energies. I've seen overworked priests and others be saved from "burnout" in their active ministries by balancing their busy outer activities of service to others with the daily practice of Centering Prayer. The Spirit renews and recharges us in the silence as we *take some time apart* to slow down into the present moment, resting in the Lord. For optimal functioning in service and for our own mental health, spiritual growth, and peace of mind we all need to find the right balance between contemplation and action in our life.

This is represented allegorically in the well-known story of "Martha the activist" and "Mary the contemplative" (Luke 10:38–42), which suggests that we each need to integrate the "Martha" and "Mary" in our soul to become whole and complete.[2]

> Contemplative prayer is a communion of love bearing Life for the multitude, to the extent that *it consents to abide in the night of faith*. The Paschal night of the Resurrection passes through the night of the agony and the tomb—the three intense moments of the Hour of Jesus which his Spirit (and not "the flesh [which] is weak") brings to life in prayer [this refers to our allegorical inner participation in Jesus' Paschal Mystery, which is an essential aspect of Centering Prayer's conceptual background[3]]. We must be willing to "keep watch with [him] one hour." (para. 2,719)

All of these quotations from the *Catechism of the Catholic Church* are consistent with the process of Centering Prayer as explained in its conceptual background—much of which is to be understood in terms of the allegorical sense of Scripture; that is, in terms of Scripture's inner meaning as related to the Holy Spirit's work of purification, healing, and transformation in our soul—which prepares us to receive the gift and grace of contemplation as described above. As to *what is* the Will of the Father, the *Catholic Catechism* tells us the following:

"It pleased God, in his goodness and wisdom, to reveal himself and make known the mystery of his will. His will was that men [and women] should have access to the Father, through Christ, the Word made flesh, in the Holy Spirit, and thus become sharers in the divine nature" (para. 51, p. 19). This is what we are implicitly asking for and consenting to in the consent of Centering Prayer.

"Now the Father's will is 'to raise up men [and women] to share in his own divine life'" (para. 541, p. 138). It's via the Spirit's work in us as we consent and cooperate in receptive contemplation and active daily life that this is to be brought about.

"Our justification comes from the grace of God. Grace is favor, the free and undeserved help that God gives us to respond to his call to become children of God, adoptive sons [and daughters], partakers of the divine nature and of eternal life" (para. 1996, p. 483).

"Grace is a participation in the life of God. It introduces us into the intimacy of the Trinitarian life" (para. 1997, p. 483). It seems clear from the above quotes that the *Catholic Catechism* is telling us that the ultimate goal of Christian Spirituality is union with God. To reach this pinnacle in the Love of Christ, our soul needs to pass through a profound process of spiritual growth that includes its inner purification, healing, and transformation by the Holy Spirit. Centering Prayer is completely in the service of this sacred process.

Hence, we have to begin in Centering Prayer from wherever we're at in our human and spiritual journey; that is, with our present limitations, resistances, and weaknesses. Yet, through time and with faithful patience, persistence, and regular daily practice, our inner obstacles will gradually be removed by the divine action to which we consciously intend to consent. Eventually, our ability to truly consent, to say "Yes" to God's Will for us, shall deepen, strengthen, and grow into a full and free consent that unites our soul's will to the Will of Divine Love in Christ—as described above in the *Catholic Catechism*. Then we shall truly receive, via the gift of silent contemplation, our divine inheritance as sons and daughters of God created in "the divine image and likeness." As the *Catechism* states, "God made us to be his sons [and daughters] through Jesus Christ according to the purpose of his will" (para. 294, p. 77). This is the rightful vocation of every Christian.

INTO TROUBLED WATERS

It's now time to enter into the troubled waters and theological divide in the Body of Christ separating contemplative Christians who practice and teach Centering Prayer from those fellow Christians who may oppose Centering Prayer and other silent contemplative methods, e.g., Dom John Main's "Christian Meditation." There has been and continues to be an intense spiritual hunger felt by many sincere

Christians longing for a deeper, more intimate relationship with Christ. In response to this longing, some have felt attracted, called, or curious about praying in simple silence—beyond the familiar faculties of memory, intellect, emotions, and creative imagination through which we've learned to pray to God. All Christians are united in our common desire to grow closer to God and to do God's Will. Let us all remember this basic aim of our common call as Christians, to follow the Gospel and grow closer to Jesus Christ.

Where we may differ and sometimes disagree is in our ideas of how to answer this call and live our faith in harmony with God's Will, and in service to the divine plan for each of us and for all of God's Creation. There are perhaps as many specific ways of pursuing this aim as there are individual souls. Yet, in all of these unique ways of following God's Will and serving the divine plan, we each need to follow, honor, and practice the same universal spiritual principles—which proceed from and are based on the Love of Christ in the heart of each soul. Jesus has indicated these principles in giving us his New Commandment that we love one another as he has loved us (John 13:34). This is a profound and radical challenge to all who would be Christ's true and faithful disciples, a challenge that goes against the grain of our natural, habitual inclinations as self-centered or group-centered human beings.

Jesus' call to spiritual discipleship challenges us to freely and willingly allow our human nature and persona to be converted by the Holy Spirit into a faithful and mature expression of the divine image in our soul—i.e., our higher spiritual nature and life in Christ (our true self). This progression of spiritual growth is outlined for us in Ephesians 4:11–24:

> And he gave some as apostles, others as prophets, others as evangelists, others as pastors and teachers, to equip the holy ones for the work of ministry, for building up the body of Christ, until we all attain to the unity of faith and knowledge of the Son of God, to mature manhood, to the extent of the full stature of Christ, from whom the whole body, joined and held together by

every supporting ligament, with the proper functioning of each part, brings about the body's growth and builds itself up in love.

So I declare and testify in the Lord that you must no longer live as the Gentiles do, in the futility of their minds; darkened in understanding, alienated from the life of God because of their ignorance, because of their hardness of heart, they have become callous and have handed themselves over to licentiousness for the practice of every kind of impurity to excess. That is not how you learned Christ, assuming you have heard of him and were taught in him, as truth is in Jesus, that you should put away the old self, corrupted through deceitful desires, and be renewed in the spirit of your minds, and put on the new self, created in God's way in righteousness and holiness of truth.

The most effective and traditional way of pursuing this end is via the receptivity and consent of "resting in God" in silent contemplative prayer—because this gives the Holy Spirit free reign to do Christ's redemptive work in us. The consent of Centering Prayer implicitly asks the Lord, our "*Maker,*" to do God's work in us; to make us into "*a new creation*" in Christ. This fulfills the moral sense of Scripture on the deepest level and it leads us into directly experiencing, over time, the allegorical sense of Scripture—which corresponds to the transformation process—within our own soul. God's transformation process clears the way for us to freely enter the spiritual sense of Scripture—i.e., *apophatic* contemplation and divine union—within our own soul.

This view of the spiritual journey is the perspective of Centering Prayer's conceptual background, as I understand it. It's based on the Scriptural Model and on Centering Prayer's basic principle of consenting to God's presence and action in us. For Christians and others who do not share this perspective (e.g., individuals who relate to God primarily in terms of the Western Model) Centering Prayer's conceptual background may seem foreign, and the idea of actually practicing Centering Prayer may make little if any sense—since it's based on our faith that God, the supreme power and ruler of Creation, is actually present in us, and is there to guide and protect us in our quest for growing intimacy in the divine relationship. Yet, we need to be spiritually prepared for this silent encounter with God, and humbly ready to experience all aspects of the hidden truth of our soul, as the Spirit may purify, heal, and rebuild us.

In personally practicing Centering Prayer for a few years—at times feeling deep inner peace, love, and a subtle awareness of God's silent presence in daily life, and at other times experiencing afflictive emotions and the dark side of my personality via the unloading of the unconscious—I could see that purification and healing were going on inside me, and that I was gradually growing closer to God in the divine relationship, but not in the ways I thought I would. This process was full of both positive and negative surprises as the divine action showed me the unexpected truth of my soul. It became, and continues to be, very interesting and has all happened in God's time and on God's terms. I noticed that friends around me, who were also practicing Centering Prayer, were experiencing the ups and downs of the spiritual journey and, happily, growing closer to God, too.

We had enough conceptual background to support one another and to understand what was going on with us.[4] There were also a few who grew impatient for results, or for whom the unloading process was too much, and so they discontinued Centering Prayer—with our blessing and encouragement to pray in the ways that they felt were right for them. I knew from my own personal experience, and from the experiences of others that Centering Prayer was effectively helping us to meet our spiritual hunger and need for a deeper, more intimate relationship with Christ. I also knew that this process of alternating "consolation and desolation" was gradually healing us in the truth of our souls, and bringing us closer to God. So I was quite surprised and disappointed to learn of the troubled waters in which some well-meaning fellow Christians were strongly criticizing and condemning Centering Prayer as "non-Christian," "Eastern Religion," "Transcendental Meditation for Christians," "New Age," "evil," and "dangerous."[5] Perhaps these individuals were unaware of the contemplative transformation process and were simply being overly cautious?

I first became aware of these anti-Centering Prayer criticisms in September of 1992; after I'd been practicing the prayer for a few years, had attended ten-day intensive and post intensive Centering Prayer Retreats (led by Thomas Keating and others), and shortly after I'd completed a several-day training retreat for presenting Introductory Centering Prayer workshops. Amid my enthusiasm for Centering Prayer and its potential for enriching Christian spirituality and the Catholic Church (which I'd returned to because of Centering Prayer), I was stunned and saddened to read over a privately circulated "dossier" (compiled by Thomas Keating, Gail Fitzpatrick-Hopler, and members of the Contemplative Outreach Staff). This dossier was put together in response to a thirteen-part series, "The New Age: Satan's Counterfeit," in which part three is an ill-informed attack condemning Centering Prayer.

This program has been broadcast repeatedly to a large and primarily Catholic audience for several years by The Eternal Word Television Network (EWTN). Thomas Keating responded to misrepresentations of Centering Prayer in the EWTN program in his article, "The Centering Prayer Method," which appeared in the fall 1992 *Contemplative Outreach Newsletter,* and is reproduced in *The Thomas Keating Reader* (pp. 34–38). Over the years (since 1992), I've met a number of Catholics and Protestants with anti-Centering Prayer prejudices who've been negatively influenced by this and other EWTN offerings concerning Centering Prayer, as I've gone about my Centering Prayer ministry. The basic objections to Centering Prayer raised by EWTN in audio, video, and written electronic formats have been addressed already in the pages of this book. It claims that 1) Centering Prayer is not really Christian prayer; 2) that Centering Prayer is dangerous and opens unsuspecting souls to evil influences; and 3) that Centering Prayer is contrary to the teachings and faith of the Catholic Church.

Given the widespread influence of the Western Model of Christian Theology; a general lack of awareness of silent *apophatic* prayer and the Christian Contemplative Tradition; limited knowledge of depth psychology (often regarded as "merely secular"); and poor understanding of the inner purification, healing, and transformation process that goes on in the soul as we grow closer to God via contemplation from our side in the divine relationship; it's not surprising that these things would be misunderstood, misinterpreted, or even feared by sincere Christians who have little or no practical knowledge of them. What is surprising (and what apparently occurred in the case of EWTN regarding Centering Prayer), is that people who teach or hold these prejudices, and who are uncomfortable with praying in silence, are sometimes unwilling to listen to what contemplatives, who are also sincere Christians, may have to say regarding their ways of praying and what Centering Prayer (or other quiet prayer) is like for them. I don't know why they didn't listen or respond to letters and requests for reconciliation (as is evident in the contents of the previously mentioned dossier). We always have a choice to open or close our hearts and minds; and one would think that Christians wanting to grow closer to God in the divine relationship would be interested in what other sincere Christians are doing that's helping them to fulfill this purpose or goal.

As stated earlier, deepening relationships require deepening levels of mutual trust. Fear and mistrust of the other are enemies of love and of understanding one another. In the Gospels, Jesus tells us repeatedly to love and forgive one another, if we mean to be his disciples (John 15:12); and: "This is how all will know that you are my disciples, if you have love for one another" (John 13:35). Love always listens to the other, and sincerely tries to understand the other. Sincere Christians are, at heart, people of love as Jesus Christ, our God, is the Lord of Love.

For many Catholic and non-Catholic Christians, EWTN is held to be a trusted and reliable source of information, teaching, inspiration, and guidance concerning their religious faith. EWTN does a lot of good and its followers, who regard it as an authoritative, trustworthy source of accurate religious teaching, seem often to accept and believe what they hear on EWTN programs without question. This statement is based on conversations I've had with regular followers of EWTN, some of whom have been influenced by anti-Centering Prayer program content over the years since I first learned of these troubled waters. I've been told such things by sincere fellow Catholics as: "We're not supposed to do that," and, "Centering Prayer is anti-Christian, dangerous, and has been debunked on EWTN." These individuals trusted the authority of EWTN and felt no need to inquire further into the issue of Centering Prayer.

The trouble and confusion regarding Centering Prayer seems to have begun around 1990 when the late Mother M. Angelica, founder and former director of EWTN, received a letter from a young woman, "Mary," who'd had some negative concerns and disturbing experiences in connection with practicing Centering Prayer. She was most likely experiencing some premature unloading of her unconscious, and was not adequately prepared for this. In any case, EWTN in connection with some conservative charismatic priests and well-meaning Catholic laywomen (see note 5 of this chapter), began an anti-Centering Prayer campaign, which has continued on EWTN and elsewhere in updated forms (see chapter 7).

Unloading the unconscious is usually not something that happens at a distance, where we may observe it objectively. It's typically so immediate, close, and subjective that we're identified and one with it in our consciousness, so that our unloading "becomes us," at least for a while. A clear example of this, combined with misdirection by an outspoken critic of Centering Prayer, is recorded in the dossier I received in 1992: A different woman, "Sue," participated in a weekly Centering Prayer group for two years. They studied *Open Mind, Open Heart* the first year and then watched the first talks of Thomas Keating's "Spiritual Journey" videos in the second year. During the first year, she "seemed to have a beginning understanding of the practice of Centering Prayer as well as started to experience a deeper sense of God's Presence and affirmation in God's love. In other words, she was experiencing the first healing effects of Centering Prayer, although she struggled with emotional fear."

This woman was also involved in the Charismatic Renewal, and became part of its ministry. A leading member of this ministry was a strongly anti-Centering Prayer critic who was the interviewer on Part Three of EWTN's series, "The New Age, Satan's Counterfeit," which is directed against Centering Prayer.[6] The woman in question likely became confused by conflicting messages regarding Centering Prayer coming from the two different prayer groups, their respective teachings, and their leaders. After her initial positive experiences in Centering Prayer, she began to notice unwanted changes in her personality; her dark side had began to surface—which is normal in the inner purification process and unloading of the unconscious. In other words, it's actually a counterintuitive sign of progress in which we're challenged to trust our "divine therapist," according to Centering Prayer's conceptual background and teachings found in the Christian Contemplative Tradition—e.g., *The Dark Night of the Soul* by John of the Cross.

Unfortunately, and probably due to the influence of her anti-Centering Prayer charismatic teacher, the woman bought into a very different interpretation of what was going on with her and Centering Prayer. She apparently felt that Centering Prayer was harming her and making her worse. As previously explained, in the unloading process, as in any deep psychotherapy, it's normal for the patient to experience getting worse *before* getting better, as the unhealthy toxic unconscious contents come up into conscious awareness to be transformed or evacuated out by passing through the person's consciousness.

The woman in question is quoted in her EWTN interview as saying, "I must have grown so intolerant to the Lord, with the pride, arrogance, haughtiness that had grown in me..." This, I believe, is a reflection of her own self-judgment concerning her previously repressed dark side—which was in dire need of acceptance, love, and healing. She also said she'd begun perceiving a lack of humility, arrogance, and pride (her own shadow qualities) in the members of her Centering Prayer group, which, of course, she ended up leaving. This was, no doubt, a projection of the repressed and shadowy unconscious contents she was, unfortunately, unwilling to take responsibility for and accept in herself. Projecting onto others, or onto God, is something we're all tempted to do when we seek "justification" or are faced with something in our self that we're afraid or unwilling to accept. From this and other examples, we may see how psychologically complex and deeply divisive are the troubled waters of opposition separating pro- and anti-Centering Prayer Christians. Our spiritual challenge in this is to forgive, trust, and accept one another as we are in the love of Christ, as Jesus tells us to do.

Based on my own personal experience, on the experiences of thousands of other long-time Centering Prayer practitioners, and on what's already been presented in this book, I feel that EWTN and others have made a serious error in condemning Centering Prayer as non-Christian, dangerous, and misleading for faithful Christians. The real and positive results in so many people's lives prove these condemnations to be untrue.[7] Individuals, groups, and organizations who promote and spread anti-Centering Prayer misinformation are, sadly, inadvertently working to prevent others, who could potentially benefit from Centering Prayer, from getting closer to God in the divine relationship. The doubt created by negative criticisms undermines trust in the Centering-Prayer process. This outcome is a true tragedy.

It's assumed and understood that the previously mentioned criticisms and condemnations of Centering Prayer were made in good faith by sincere Christians who believed they were defending the Catholic Faith and looking out for the spiritual wellbeing of others. This is what makes it so sad and tragic. The Western Theological Model, combined with negative reports from a few individuals, plus a lack of accurate knowledge regarding Centering Prayer, its transformation process, and regarding our rich Christian Contemplative Heritage, have, no doubt, all contributed to forming the conclusions of Centering Prayer's critics and detractors. When Contemplative Prayer was not part of their religious education, they don't know better.

Thus, it is understandable that sincere Catholics and Protestants may have doubts and concerns regarding Centering Prayer, due to the unconscious influence of the Western Model, and due to mistrust of praying in a new way that was not part of their original religious training; though, at least for Catholics, the Church's *Catechism* and other important voices clearly state that contemplative prayer (for which Centering Prayer prepares us) is and always has been an integral part of deepening prayer and spirituality in the Catholic Christian Tradition. The gift of *apophatic* contemplation, though unfortunately not well known these days, is, in fact, the climatic movement of our soul into God and of God into our soul. The "other important voices" that affirm contemplative prayer and the spiritual growth process it engenders include: Holy Scripture; doctors and mystics of the Church such as Saint Augustine; Gregory the Great; Meister Eckhart; Teresa of Avila; John of the Cross; and Thomas Merton; Vatican II's call to renew the contemplative dimension of the Gospel[8]; and Pope John XXIII, who said, "Contemplation should be the goal of all Christians by virtue of our call to perfection" (cf. "Be perfect as your heavenly Father is perfect," Matt. 5:48).

We long to find peace, reconciliation, and unity with our beloved Christian brothers and sisters who may oppose Centering Prayer without knowing its true value for many of us. We're confident that if they'll try to see what we're doing in practicing Centering Prayer, as we trust and understand it—and as expressed in the foregoing pages—that there need be no further confusion or problems regarding this. We always have a choice to open or close our hearts and minds. Jesus enjoins us to love and forgive one another; and to become one bread and body in the Love of Christ. In Matthew 7:20, Jesus tells us, "You will know them by their fruits." If we look to the fruits produced in the lives of people who've practiced Centering Prayer regularly for some time, and for whom it is appropriate, we shall see abundant evidence of this simple prayer's value as a vehicle for the work of the Holy Spirit in human souls (see note 7 of this chapter).

THE BIG TENT

A few years ago at a ministry fair at Holy Family Cathedral in Anchorage, Alaska, where I had a Centering Prayer table, a devout woman, who'd been influenced by negative claims regarding Centering Prayer, said to me and the Pastor, Fr. Anthony Patalano, O.P., that I shouldn't be allowed to have a table there or a prayer group at the Cathedral (which I'd had for several years). Fr. Anthony replied that the Catholic Church is a "Big Tent," there's room for all ways of praying under this "Tent," and that contemplative prayer, i.e., Centering Prayer, is legitimate Christian prayer. I'd given Fr. Anthony a copy of Thomas Keating's book, *The Mystery of Christ*, several years earlier and was grateful for his support now.

The *Catholic Catechism* speaks to a variety of souls under its "Big Tent." The beginning teachings, given to children, reflect the Western Model and stress a God Who loves us and is always around us. These teachings are grounded in traditional rational theology. Beyond basic rational theology is a deeper mystical theology, which is intuitive, nondual, and affirms our union with God in the Love of Christ (the spiritual sense of Scripture). Many people under the Big Tent are in stages of rational theology that do not recognize the mystical stages into which Centering Prayer and the gift of *apophatic* contemplation may lead us. From this theological gap have come the theological divide and the troubled waters across it. Everyone under the Big Tent belongs to the Body of Christ and should follow in prayer, belief, and action what they feel in their heart is right and true for them; and everyone under the Big Tent needs to honor and respect the rights of all sincere Christians to pray and believe in the ways that they feel are right for them—even if we don't understand what some of our beloved fellow Christian brothers and sisters are doing or why.

There are so many ways of praying or relating to God in the divine relationship. We need to engage the divine relationship on all levels of our being in order to have a fully engaged and integrated relationship with God. Hence, Centering Prayer practitioners do not give up their other ways of praying and worshipping the Lord—e.g., vocal prayer, meditation, and sacred ritual. The best ways for each of us to pray are those that fit our particular needs in our present stage of spiritual growth in relation to God. The Big Tent welcomes and has room for people in all stages or levels of relationship to God; that is, acquaintanceship, friendliness, friendship, and full intimacy or union of life (as discussed in chapter 3). Every way of praying is good because each honors our Creator and acknowledges the divine relationship we have with God. Our spiritual journey is a gradual movement from human ground into spiritual ground; that is, it's a movement from our humanly perceived separations from God into the wondrous discovery of God's intimate gift of silent contemplation and growing union in the Love of Christ. Divine Love is the core key and great equalizing factor uniting us all in the Body of Christ, our true spiritual ground. Our practical participation in God's Love is far more important, immediate, and valuable than are our humanly created theological beliefs or intellectual understanding, which are of a more abstract, theoretical nature.

Just as the Church is a Big Tent with room for all ways of praying and relating to God, so are there many ways into the gift of contemplation that God invites us to receive, so we may be brought closer into the intimacy of the divine relationship. God longs to share God's Love with each of us through the gift of contemplation. It is for this loving purpose that we were created in the divine image and likeness (Gen. 1:26–27) by the one true God Who "*is love,*" (1 John 4:8, 16). If a person is unaware of *what* the gift of contemplation actually is, then he or she may not know to consent and accept this most precious gift when it's offered by the Holy Spirit. The good woman mentioned in chapter 4 (pp. 89–90), who God was "putting on 'automatic pilot,'" is an example of someone who didn't know to welcome and accept the Spirit's quiet gift of a deepening prayer and relationship until she heard about Centering Prayer and the gift of contemplation. She'd had no idea what it was because she'd never been told about it. Hence, she didn't know to trust the urge to be still when it came to her in her *kataphatic* prayer.

The Holy Spirit's invitation into silent contemplation could come in the midst of any form of *kataphatic* Christian prayer or worship—e.g., praying the Holy Rosary, Adoration of the Blessed Sacrament, *Lectio Divina*, Novenas, or Charismatic Worship. This may happen when one spontaneously experiences an inclination to slow down, stop, and pause into the immediate present moment beyond the prayerful activities of the faculties (memory, intellect, emotions, or imagination) and the physical body. One is gently drawn inward and effortlessly sinks into the rest of a simple silence beyond words, thoughts, images, feelings, and bodily movements. If someone does not know that this is an invitation into a deeper level of prayer on the level of being and resting in God, then he or she may misunderstand and unwittingly say "No" to the Holy Spirit's invitation to enter into the gift of quiet, *apophatic* contemplation; as was the case with the prayerful woman mentioned in chapter 4.

There's an important link between Charismatic Prayer and *apophatic* Contemplative Prayer that sometimes occurs. When the faculties are overwhelmed or suspended by the Holy Spirit in Charismatic Worship, then one may spontaneously "rest in the Spirit" or be "slain in the Spirit." This experience, in which a person appears to lose consciousness or "fall asleep," is a beginning contemplative state that requires a certain level of trust, openness, and receptivity on the part of the individual receiving this mysterious gift. Similar levels of trust, openness, and receptivity are needed in the consent of Centering Prayer. In both cases, this receptivity may be an entryway into an *apophatic* contemplative state, though the experience may be interpreted differently by individuals practicing these two very different prayer forms. Additional differences lie in what they're doing prior to entering the rest of this silent inner absorption; as well as in the outer settings in which this is experienced.

That is, with Charismatic Worship, one may be quite emotionally engaged and active while worshipping in a communal setting where others are doing the same things (e.g., praising the Lord, speaking in tongues, giving testimony, feeling the inspiring energy of the Holy Spirit, and so on). This is, of course, prior to experiencing "resting" or being "slain in the Spirit." With Centering Prayer practice, on the other hand, one is outwardly quiet, detaching from *all kataphatic* phenomena, and usually praying privately in solitude. Outwardly, Charismatic Worship and Centering Prayer appear to be the opposite of each other. Inwardly, they may overlap slightly.

The conceptual backgrounds or theoretical explanations of these two prayer forms also differ significantly, to the point where the idea of silent contemplation may be unfamiliar to charismatic worshippers. Yet, both Charismatic Worship and Centering Prayer may lead into similar beginning states of resting in God. This is interesting to note because some of Centering Prayer's strongest critics have been practitioners of Charismatic Prayer and Worship.[9] In *Open Mind, Open Heart*, Thomas Keating writes of Charismatic Prayer as being one preliminary way of preparing the soul for quiet *apophatic* contemplation, especially in terms of the gift of tongues (pp. 133–135).

Because of where they may both inwardly take us, Centering Prayer and Charismatic Worship are not necessarily incompatible; they may, in some cases, actually complement each other—if a person finds both to be spiritually nourishing and enriching. For example, I know a devout Hispanic woman who practices Centering Prayer daily and also facilitates a weekly Hispanic Charismatic Prayer group. She is enriched by both of these prayer practices. When we're faithful and sincere, God will reach out to us within the parameters of however we pray. Our responsibility is to be open, attentive, pliable, and responsive to the subtle movements of the Holy Spirit within us, and willing to let go of our preconceived prayer agendas when the Spirit suggests we do so. In receptively sensing and faithfully following the Spirit's inner guidance in prayer and action, we may be led by the Holy Spirit into deeper prayer and intimacy in the divine relationship. "You are guided by the Spirit" (Gal. 5:18).

God is calling us all into Divine Light, Life, and Love, regardless of how we may prefer to pray and relate to God. All sincere prayer is good. As Christians, we need to recognize this and to honor the needs and rights of everyone to pray in the ways that they feel are appropriate for them. Ultimately, the Lord longs to bring us all into the same spiritual place. As the late great Canadian poet and songwriter, Leonard Cohen, so prophetically exclaims, "Every heart, every heart to love will come; but like a refugee."[10] To me, this says it all in simple language. We're all destined to seek and find refuge in our true spiritual home: the Love of God.

The gift of contemplation, of God's presence and action in our soul, is our way home into this love. It does not matter very much *how* we get there; that is, how we're drawn into God's Rest. The important thing is that, when separations and divides are experienced or perceived, we do get there by saying "Yes" to this most precious and intimate gift of the Holy Spirit. May we say "Yes," again and again, whenever and however the Lord's Rest is offered us in the deepening gentle silence of human life and spiritual awakening. There, in the Lord, we shall finally come to know that we are all one as human beings and spiritual beings, united in the Love of Christ.

7

CALMING THE TROUBLED WATERS

THE CALMING GIFTS

Knowledge, Understanding, and Wisdom are the contemplative gifts of the Spirit arising in the soul out of the spiritual sense of Scripture (God's Word, Christ in us).[1] These holy gifts of great peace calm the turbulent waters of confusion, strife, and enmity caused by fear, anger, and ignorance—the divisive creations of hatred, lies, and slavery (Evil). Love, Truth, and Freedom are the spiritual antidotes to all hatred, lies, and slavery in created reality. These sacred antidotes calm all troubled waters in the soul and in human relationships.

The troubled waters related to Centering Prayer are stirred up by worry, doubt, mistrust, and misunderstanding of the Holy Spirit's mysterious process of healing and renewal in the soul—what goes on *"in secret"* in the prayer of consent to God's action. We call this prayer *"apophatic* contemplation" (cf. Matt. 6:6). If our hearts will open softly and respond willingly to love, then we shall come to *"know the truth"* of our soul, and this knowing "shall set us free" (cf. John 8:32). Love in the soul draws all things to its self and makes them one. By giving love, truth, and freedom to others, we gain them for ourselves.

We give love by seeing, valuing, and responding in solidarity to the intrinsic worth of every soul in God; we give truth by being honest in our dealings and communications with others; and we give freedom by allowing others to make their own informed decisions, and by encouraging others to freely discover and be who they truly are as human beings and spiritual beings. This is deeply calming and conducive to peace, understanding, and love in human souls and relationships. It grows from a personal responsibility in each soul that's grounded in a firm will toward God and Goodness.

POINTS FOR CENTERING PRAYER

We know that Centering Prayer is not appropriate for everyone under the Big Tent, though it's open and available to everyone. Some individuals are not comfortable with or prepared for silent prayer and opening to the energies of the unconscious. Others of us, in desiring a deeper relationship with God, do feel an attraction to quiet prayer. For such individuals, Centering Prayer may be a good fit as a practical, simple way for opening to the gift of nonconceptual contemplation. Being faithful to Centering Prayer practice requires a daily commitment (as on the friendship level of relationship) that not everyone is ready or willing to make. Such a commitment needs inner motivation inspired by a heartfelt hunger for a deeper relationship with God. The spiritual hunger to patiently persist in the daily discipline of Centering Prayer is a gift and call from the Holy Spirit into silent, receptive prayer. Not everyone feels this call; and among those of us who do, not everyone answers it.

Some sincere Christians who've not felt called to silent prayer, or who've been misinformed about it, may question the validity of Centering Prayer. In addition to what's already been detailed in this book, a briefer response may be simply to appeal to the words of Jesus in Matthew 7:17, 20, where He says: "Every good tree bears good fruit, but the bad tree bears bad fruit... You will know them by their fruits." If we look to the kinds of fruits produced in the lives and souls of individuals who've appropriately and faithfully practiced Centering Prayer for some years, and who've followed Thomas Keating's teachings, we'll see ample evidence of the Gospel values, fruits, and gifts of the Spirit, and movements toward the service of others in all areas of human life. There are also numerous individual video testimonials as to the human and spiritual benefits of Centering Prayer posted on the Contemplative Outreach website (www.contemplativeoutreach.org) under "Voices of Grace and Gratitude."

When Pope Francis visited the United States in September 2015, I was fortunate to listen to his address to the United States Congress on National Public Radio. Near the end of his talk, the Pope mentioned the four deceased Americans whose life and work he most admires. They are: Abraham Lincoln, Dorothy Day, Martin Luther King, and Thomas Merton. Pope Francis stated that he "admires Thomas Merton's contemplative way." I was delighted to hear this from the leader of the Catholic Church! It affirmed for me the Pope's support of "renewing the contemplative dimension of the Gospel," which is essentially what Centering Prayer—following in the wake of Vatican II and from the work of Thomas Merton—is here to help do.

TWO VATICAN DOCUMENTS

There are two important documents from the Catholic Church regarding prayer and "New Age" practices that have been cited (incorrectly) by relatively recent critics of Centering Prayer as "evidence" that Centering Prayer is non-Christian and contrary to Church teaching.[2] The first of these documents, "Letter to the Bishops of the Catholic Church on Some Aspects of Christian Meditation" (1989), appeared in *Vatican Translation* in English in the early 1990s, published in America by the Daughters of St. Paul. This document was issued by the Congregation for the Doctrine of the Faith (CDF), under the direction of Joseph Cardinal Ratzinger (who later became Pope Benedict XVI). As Thomas Keating points out in his article, "Clarifications Regarding Centering Prayer":

> [Cardinal Ratzinger's] "Letter to the Bishops...on Some Aspects of Christian Meditation" was not directed to Centering Prayer...but rather at those forms of meditative practice that actually incorporate the methods of Eastern meditations such as Zen and the use of Hindu mantras. The letter is chiefly concerned with the integration of such techniques into the

Christian faith. It does not forbid their use and indeed, states, "That does not mean that genuine practices of meditation which come from the Christian East and from the great non-Christian religions... cannot constitute a suitable means of helping the person who prays to come before God with an interior peace even in the midst of external pressures" (no. 28).

Fr. Keating continues:

> Having noted this affirmation of the value of the Eastern prac-
> tices when rightly integrated into Christian faith, may I point
> out that Centering Prayer is the one contemporary form of con-
> templative practice that *does not* make use of any of these tech-
> niques? The quotation from the Letter that the gift of contem-
> plation can only be granted through the Holy Spirit is precisely
> what we teach.[3]

Upon proper examination, and with an accurate understanding of actual Centering Prayer practice and its background within the Christian Contemplative Tradition, it becomes clear that the CDF's "Some Aspects of Christian Meditation" does not negate the validity of Centering Prayer as legitimate Christian prayer, but actually affirms it. For whatever reasons, some critics of Centering Prayer disagree with this and have interpreted this document differently, and concluded differently, (see next section, "Old Wine and New Wineskins").

Reasoning from surface appearances, and without a thorough knowledge of Centering Prayer and where it actually comes from, some sincere Catholic critics have come to mistaken conclusions regarding the prayer and the CDF's "Letter on Some Aspects of Christian Meditation." The same is true with reference to the second important Vatican Document that misinformed critics have cited as "evidence" against the validity of Centering Prayer as authentic Catholic Christian Prayer. This second document was created by the Pontifical Councils for Culture and Interreligious Dialogue. They refer to this detailed study as "a provisional report," meaning it is not a finalized document. The title is: "Jesus Christ the Bearer of the Water of Life: A Christian Reflection on the 'New Age.'" (This 56-page article may be viewed in its entirety online by searching its title and then selecting the Vatican website). This document actually supports the legitimacy of Centering Prayer under the Big Tent of the Christian Church, when Centering Prayer and its historical and conceptual backgrounds are accurately understood.

In 2006, I was invited to teach a six-week introduction to Centering Prayer as part of the adult education program at a local Catholic Church. About nine people came, all of them well-educated conservative Catholics curious about contemplative prayer. A few of them had encountered negative criticisms regarding Centering Prayer as a "New Age" counterfeit of true Christian Spirituality; and we had some lively discussions.

One of the men in the group found "Jesus Christ the Bearer of the Water of Life" in the archives of the Vatican website. In addition to studying Thomas Keating's *Open Mind, Open Heart*, we decided to study this Vatican article, as a basis for interpreting what the Church might think of Centering Prayer. After reviewing and discussing the article, we all agreed that there's nothing to be found in it that could call Centering Prayer, as presented in *Open Mind, Open Heart*, into question as a legitimate prayer practice for Catholic Christians.

The Pontifical Councils for Culture and Interreligious Dialogue have created a detailed and impressive provisional document regarding the "New Age" movements. It's scholarly, well researched, and quite clear in articulating various "New Age" spiritualities in relation to Catholic Doctrine. Below are some basic points supporting Centering Prayer that I addressed to my class members in regards to this document. These points may be helpful in responding to questions, doubts, and criticisms that confuse Centering Prayer and its conceptual background with non-Christian "New Age" practices and ideas: The Vatican Report, part 3.4 ("Christian Mysticism and New Age Mysticism"), part 3.5 ("The God within and *theosis*"), and part 4 ("New Age and Christian Faith in Contrast") are especially relevant to questions regarding Centering Prayer and "New Age" spiritual movements.

One class member raised the issue of Pantheism. Monistic *Pantheism* (Greek for "everything is God") identifies God with and limits God to created reality. It tends to be impersonal, non-relational, and agnostic. Christian faith, on the other hand, affirms each unique soul's personal and intimate relationship with God through Christ, and understands God (the Ultimate Mystery and Ultimate Reality) as both one with and fully aware of God's entire creation while simultaneously transcending creation and abiding in God's self beyond creation ("in unapproachable light," 1 Tim. 6:16). This theological notion of Christian faith integrates the Western and Scriptural Models and is much closer to the idea of *Pan-en-theism* than it is to Pantheism. Panentheism has been suggested by Thomas Keating as a perspective for Centering Prayer's conceptual background, *not Pantheism*—which limits God to the Universe of created reality.[4] The following diagrams suggest the differences among dualistic Theism (Western Model), Monistic Pantheism, and Non-Dual Panentheism (Scriptural Model):

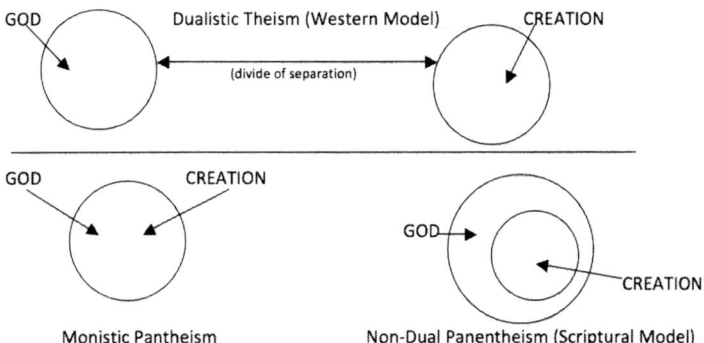

Theological Monism "allows for no distinction between God and creation."[5] Monism is the binary opposite of Theism (the Western Model)—which places God outside of creation and the soul. Some critics of Centering Prayer have mistakenly concluded that the prayer, as taught by Thomas Keating, assumes a non-Christian theological Monism.[6] However, Monistic Pantheism is not the only monotheistic (belief in One God) option to the dualistic Theism of the Western Model. The insights of Panentheism (a more evolved and nuanced concept) may bridge across and calm the troubled waters of contradiction and conflict between dualistic Theism and monistic Pantheism; since Panentheism transcends, includes, and integrates these two opposite perspectives. Centering Prayer's critics do not appear to appreciate the theological idea of Pan-en-theism and its profound implications. Non-dual Panentheism is affirmed in the Scriptures by the vision of God as including "Our Father in heaven" (Matt. 6:9); "Your Father who sees in secret" (Matt. 6:6); and "Him in whom we live and move and have our being" (Acts 17:28).

Let's now look at some points contrasting Centering Prayer with "New Age" teachings and practices as described in the Vatican Document, "Jesus Christ the Bearer of the Water of Life" (which contains no mention of Centering Prayer):

1) New Age teachings stress self-reliance to the point that you can do the spiritual journey all by yourself. In the Christian spirituality of Centering Prayer, we are utterly dependent on the mercy of God and the love of Christ to bring us to divine union. *Centering Prayer works by God's grace and not by our efforts*, though some efforts on our own part (e.g., taking time each day to be faithful to the prayer and consenting to the divine action) are necessary to create the conditions in us to allow God's grace to work.

2) Centering Prayer (as explained in chapter 5) is not a technique, as are the various New Age practices referenced in the Vatican Document. Reliable techniques produce specific results when done properly. Centering Prayer is a method that does not produce specific results but leaves the results open to whatever the divine action may choose for us as we let go and consent. This prayer is a partnership with Christ in which we trust that the Holy Spirit will do in us, in God's time, what is actually needed to bring us closer in the divine relationship. Centering Prayer is an act of humble faith and intimate trusting that, by virtue of our consent, the Holy Spirit is working in us, "*in secret*," regardless of what the conscious psychological content of our

experience may be during the time of Centering Prayer. This is a fundamental principle of Centering Prayer and our cooperation with the divine action.

3) Centering Prayer is a "transformative spirituality" rather than a "feel-good spirituality" for our ego or false-self persona (as are some of the "New Age" spiritual movements). As previously discussed, this transformation process is initiated and carried out by the grace of God's presence and action in us. Engaging the inner work of this spiritual process in the soul is our allegorical participation in Jesus' Paschal Mystery, leading ultimately to the freedom of inner resurrection and ascension into the Father's heavenly kingdom of Divine Love. Thomas Keating has said that being faithful to our daily Centering Prayer practice and willingness to be transformed by the Holy Spirit are all that's required of us to do our part in cooperation with God's work in our soul. This, of course, assumes that we're fulfilling the moral sense of Scripture as best we can by living a life based on the Gospel Values.

4) At its worst, "feel-good" New Age spirituality seeks and promises to satisfy the emotional happiness programs of the false-self system discussed in chapter 1. The Christian spirituality of Centering Prayer is aimed at freeing us from the mistaken identity of our false self and from its unconscious happiness programs. Centering Prayer is not part of any non-Christian, New Age spirituality, but a sincere effort to bring the Gospel of Jesus Christ into practical manifestation in our souls and our society. Anyone who has an accurate understanding of Centering Prayer and its background, and who reads and reflects on the provisional Vatican Report, "Jesus Christ the Bearer of the Water of Life," will clearly see that Centering Prayer is not a "New Age" practice, as some confused critics have maintained. Centering Prayer is a valid expression of Catholic Christian Prayer and the Christian Contemplative Tradition that's come down to us from the time of Jesus and the origins of Christianity.

Old Wine and New Wineskins

Jesus gives a teaching parable in Matthew 9:17 that may help us to calm the troubled waters and bridge the divide between those who follow Centering Prayer and those who oppose it: "People do not put new wine into old wineskins. Otherwise the skins burst, the wine spills out, and the skins are ruined. Rather, they pour new wine into fresh wineskins, and both are preserved." Variations of this important parable also appear in the Gospels of Mark (2:22) and Luke (5:37–39).

There are various ways of interpreting and learning from God's Word in the allegorical sense of Scripture. This is an essential aspect of the spiritual richness and creative genius of God's Word. That is, the allegorical meaning of Scripture has potential relevance to us in *all* the stages of our spiritual growth. As we change and evolve, the Scripture's inner meaning and our hearing of it change and evolve correspondingly.

Thomas Keating gives an insightful interpretation of Jesus' parable about the old and new wine and wineskins.[7] He refers to the "New Wine" as "a marvelous image of the Holy Spirit," saying, "the energy of the Spirit cannot be contained in the old structures." In its boundless creativity, the Spirit is continually doing new things (Isa. 43:19), and renewing God's creation (Rev. 21:5). The idea of "new wine" in "new wineskins" compares well to the idea that a living spiritual tradition—e.g., Contemplative Christianity, needs to be updated and renewed in each successive generation, if it's to keep up with the changing times and conditions of evolving human knowledge, language, culture, and consciousness. If it fails to do so, it will lose its practical relevance for many people in society; but not for all of them.

Some people, who we may call "conservatives" or "traditionalists," are not comfortable with new innovations or changes and prefer to rely on the older, proven ways of doing things. In terms of Jesus' parable, we may say that conservative traditionalists prefer the "old wine" in its "old wineskins" and may be resistant to or distrustful of any "new wine" or "new wineskins."[8] These good folks, it seems to me, are today's critics of Centering Prayer and its conceptual background; or at least those aspects of it that are new evolving innovations and expressions of the ancient Christian Contemplative Tradition. Interestingly, and this is a key point that Centering Prayer's detractors and critics seem to miss, Centering Prayer's presentation and conceptual background include and emerge out of the "old wine" and "old wineskins" of the Christian Contemplative Tradition. They do this in such a way as to carry the treasures of the "old wine" and "old wineskins" forward from the past into the present and future as "new wine" in "new wineskins," thus remaining potentially relevant to everyone while preserving the past *and* keeping step with the evolving changes in human knowledge, culture, and society. Realizing and understanding the truth of this may serve to calm our troubled waters.

Conservative, "old wineskin" Christians may have difficulty relating to or accepting spiritual teaching and truths that are not expressed in the older forms of biblical and traditional language (with which they're familiar and identify). They may feel that newer, innovative expressions of the Christian Gospel and Contemplative Tradition are really not part of the authentic Christian Tradition. For example, the wonderful quote that humans are created in God's image and likeness (Gen. 1:26–27) comes directly out of the Scriptures to which both traditionalist and nontraditionalist (i.e., modern, postmodern, and integral) Christians relate. When Thomas Keating expresses the same fundamental spiritual truth in more modern language, saying that all humans are born with and have within them "the divine DNA," traditionalists may have trouble relating to or accepting this contemporary metaphor; since it's new, not in the Bible, and has not come down to us from the venerable past. This is their prerogative.

It does not make the traditionalists wrong. Everyone has a right to be who they are or choose to be. In Luke 5:38–39, Jesus' parable about the old and new wine concludes by saying, "Rather, new wine must be poured into fresh wineskins. [And] no one who has been drinking old wine desires new, for he says, 'The old is good.'" If we think of the old wine allegorically as the Lord's Rest, the gift of *apophatic* contemplation that brings us into communion and union with the Holy Spirit; then what more could we ask for? Indeed this "old wine" is exceedingly good; that is, for all who are able to access it in the "old wineskins" of the venerable past—i.e., those conservative contemplatives who are traditionalists. On the other hand, for those who are not able to freely access the gift of *apophatic* contemplation by way of the "old wine" in its "old wineskins," "new wine" in "new wineskins" may be what's required. In this context, where the wine represents the gift of infused *apophatic* contemplation (the divine presence and action in the soul), there's really no difference between the "old wine" and the "new wine." Essentially, they are both the same identical thing. If Centering Prayer practitioners and their traditionalist critics can humbly realize this and peacefully respect and love one another (as Jesus commands us to do in John 15:17), this will greatly help to calm the sad, troubled waters between us.

The difference between "old wine" and "new wine" actually lies in the *kataphatic* containers or structures ("wineskins") through which sincere Christians may access the precious wine (gift) of the Holy Spirit's presence and action in us. If we access this sacred wine via its "old wineskins"—i.e., the language, structures, and ways of the past, then we may call it "old wine." If we access it via a "new wineskin," then we may call it "new wine." The secret *apophatic* contemplative gift of the Holy Spirit transcends time and all "wineskins," so there's really no difference between the old and the new wines of the past and the present; once we're actually in the "now wine" of God's living presence and action in our soul. The *kataphatic* forms or structures through which we may pray to access this holy gift are created for our use in time and space by the inspiration of the Holy Spirit in the souls of those who offer them to us. Hence, we may refer to them as "old wineskins" or "new wineskins," based on the times and places of their origins and use. There's really no conflict between them, provided they actually do bring us into accessing the true wine and gift of *apophatic* contemplation.

Troubled waters arise when practitioners of the "old wineskins" misunderstand, distrust, and oppose practitioners of the "new wineskins"—that is, Conservative Traditionalists versus Centering Prayer practitioners. Troubled waters also arise if Centering Prayer practitioners of the "new wineskins" reject those of the "old wineskins" as being "out of date" with contemporary times. There's room for both under the Big Tent of Christ's Church.

The wineskins are useful containers that hold the sacred wine and guide us to it. The Holy Spirit is extremely adaptable and may not be limited to only one container. The wineskins are *kataphatic* guides serving as spiritual maps for our inner journey into God. The living wine of the true and most righteous Gospel itself is *apophatic*—beyond all categories, symbols, concepts, and *kataphatic* forms or experiences—e.g., spiritual visions or charismatic gifts. So long as our maps (wineskins) are true and trustworthy, there is more than one exclusive route to reach our soul's ultimate destination. Yet all true maps, all worthy wineskins must adhere to the same Divine Law and Universal Spiritual Principles of love, truth, and freedom for all souls. Otherwise, they may lead us astray like lost sheep in the land of the wolf. This seems to be what anti-Centering Prayer critics most fear about this contemporary contemplative method; that it will lead innocent, unknowing souls astray into "the land of the wolf." Happily, the actual lived experiences of thousands of long-time Centering Prayer practitioners, for whom Centering Prayer is appropriate, prove beyond doubt that this is not the case at all.

WHY THE PROBLEMS?

Some practitioners of Centering Prayer may wonder why the prayer and its conceptual background are so misunderstood and rejected as authentic Christian prayer by its critics. One simple answer to this is that new spiritual wine and wineskins cannot be accurately perceived through the viewing lens of the old wineskins. Traditionalists, and those in earlier stages of evolving consciousness—i.e., the warrior and tribal stages[9]—interpret Christianity (or any religion) primarily through traditional language, concepts, and the binary perspectives of the Western Model (God-outside-the-soul and the-soul-outside-of-God).

In developing the Method of Centering Prayer and its conceptual background, Thomas Keating and others have translated the Christian Contemplative Tradition into contemporary language, and enriched it by drawing from and integrating important insights from modern depth psychology, other social sciences, and the physical sciences. These are discoveries and insights about human nature, history, society, and physical reality that were generally unknown in previous times. This is not a departure from the ancient tradition of Christian spirituality that's come down to us from the past, but a vital continuation of it that furthers its evolving revelation in our time; preserving and reverencing the living transmission of authentic Christian contemplative spirituality from the past (the "old wine" and "wineskins"), while giving us "new wine" in "new wineskins." The Method of Centering Prayer and its conceptual background are a work in progress that includes and integrates *both* the old and the new.

We cannot really see the new through the eyes of the old, nor the old through the eyes of the new. If we try to, what we'll get will be a distorted picture and misinterpretation of something that can't fit or be rightly seen through the viewing frame of our basic assumptions and preconceptions. To see and grasp the "new" as it actually is, we need to go "outside the box" of our current assumptions and preconceptions, and be willing to learn and adopt, at least temporarily, a new set of assumptions and preconceptions. We need to be willing to try thinking in a new way. Only thus may we begin to see and understand the new (or the old) in terms of its true frame of reference. Not everyone is willing or able to do this.

In the case of Centering Prayer, more than thinking about it is needed. That is, it's necessary to actually practice the prayer daily over an extended period of time, and thus experience firsthand its effects in oneself and one's life in the context of the divine relationship, before it's possible to truly appreciate and understand what this prayer really is. We can't really know it by judging from outside, thinking or speculating about it—as some of Centering Prayer's critics have done.

New terms and concepts are invented to express the true wine of the past in new language and thought patterns (wineskins) that carry the living ancient tradition forward into the present collective environment of our contemporary civilization, society, and experiences. The basic principles of universal love, truth, and freedom never change—as God or non-created Reality is the one eternal constant— the Ultimate Wineskin—holding everything together; but the ways in which God's infinite truths are expressed (the smaller wineskins) do change to fit the diverse new circumstances in which the Holy Spirit (the true wine of Christ's Vine) is manifesting itself.

This simple fact of created reality is something that "old wine-skin" conservatives and critics of Centering Prayer may have trouble appreciating or accepting. In such cases, they tend to hold to one side of the theological divide, to become overly defensive, and to stir up troubled waters by resisting and rejecting the "new wine" in its "new wineskins." If the "old wine" in its "old wineskins" is working well for them, then they have every right and are wise to keep to the time-tested ways of the past that are serving them so well as they grow closer to God in the divine relationship via the gift of infused *apophatic* contemplation. Yet, they need to realize that theirs is not the only true way to God that *everyone else* must follow to be "saved."

The Holy Spirit is extremely creative, versatile, and adaptable; and there's room for *all* ways of praying (relating to God) under the Big Tent of Christ's Universal Church. Let our beloved traditionalists and critics be reassured that they have nothing to fear or reject in the "new wine" of Centering Prayer in its "new wineskins," so long as this new wine remains true to the Spirit by expressing the same universal principles that inspired their "old wine" in its "old wineskins." We are referring here to the eternal spiritual values and principles of Divine Love, Truth, and Freedom yearning and crying out for fulfillment in the heart of every soul.

"THE JURY IS IN!"

Thomas Keating has said that resting in silent contemplation is a natural state of being for all humans to spontaneously enter into, whether we consciously think of it as prayer or as something else. Having good rest in our lives counteracts and balances out the natural stresses of activity on all levels of our being: physical, vital, emotional, mental, psychic, social, and spiritual. Adequate rest is essential for human health and wellbeing in all of us.

The deep rest of contemplative prayer, as given by God to the soul, is the most profound, enriching, and refreshing rest that we may experience—though the process also involves the unloading of the unconscious, which can be temporarily stressful and anything but relaxing. Ultimately, the unloading process leads to healing in the soul and a deeper rest than was possible before. Some "old wineskin" critics of Centering Prayer, following the teaching of earlier times regarding the progressive stages of prayer, feel that it's necessary to work through the earlier stages of prayer before one can be ready for the gift of contemplation.[10] They may disagree with the egalitarian claim that Centering Prayer is potentially open to everyone in every stage of prayer and spiritual development.

They may disagree because beginning with Centering Prayer does not appear to them to jibe with the teachings of earlier times. We cannot say that they're wrong here because there definitely are progressive steps on the ladder of prayer, as Teresa of Avila points out in her writings.[11] However, when someone comes to Centering Prayer, there's a very high probability that he or she will already have been practicing various *kataphatic* prayer forms; such as vocal prayer, mental prayer, affective prayer, or charismatic prayer; and will continue to practice these kinds of prayer. Centering Prayer does not replace other ways of praying, but simply adds a deeper dimension to our prayer life. Critics often seem to miss this point.

It may be helpful to humbly remember that we cannot judge from outside who may or may not be spiritually ready to receive the mysterious gift of the Lord's Rest in *apophatic* contemplation. Only God, the giver of this gift, knows this. God's gift of the Lord's Rest may be offered to anyone whenever the divine action chooses to do so. This gift, like the Holy Spirit, is free and not bound by our rules or preconceptions. As mentioned earlier, Centering Prayer (which prepares our faculties to receive this gift) is safe and suitable for most people in today's world who are: 1) in reasonably good mental health; 2) desire a deeper, more intimate relationship with God; and 3) who feel inclined to praying quietly in receptive silence. Centering Prayer is definitely not right for everyone, but whoever feels curious or interested should feel free and not frightened to give it a try. Without trust in prayer or among humans, there can be no meaningful relationship.

Today, most of us are living in very different conditions than the Christians of earlier times. Our modern pace of life and technology-driven environments are much busier than those of times past. So it seems natural that the Holy Spirit, in wanting to share the precious gift of God's intimate presence and action with human souls, would make silent contemplation available to as many people as possible through a practice like Centering Prayer. We ought to be open to the fact that the Holy Spirit is so creatively adaptable and delights in doing "new things." If one is curious about this prayer or feels inclined to try it, the only practical, hands-on way to find out if it's right for you is to give it a "trial run" by practicing it daily—twice each day for twenty minutes—for six to eight weeks. Then you'll be in a good position to decide if it's right for you at this time.

Many thousands of people have given Centering Prayer a "trial run," and "the jury is in." People have been practicing Centering Prayer under the direction of Contemplative Outreach (founded 1984) for well over thirty years, and we may now confidently affirm that this prayer is safe, appropriate, and highly beneficial for most sincere Christians who are eager and willing to commit themselves to growing in and deepening the divine relationship through the discipline of daily Centering Prayer, combined with the action of living a life based on the Gospel values in service to those around them. If Centering

Prayer were as dangerous and contrary to the Catholic Church or Christian Faith as some of its early critics maintained, Contemplative Outreach and the growing numbers of daily Centering Prayer practitioners throughout the world would not be flourishing as they are today. The results are in and the truth stands revealed for all who're willing to see it.

Centering Prayer is decidedly good for the mental health, spiritual growth, and wellbeing of all those Christians for whom it is appropriate. This is not a matter of speculation or opinion. It's a matter of true, demonstrated fact that's here for anyone to see who is willing to honestly look at the reality of the situation. The negative opinions, assumptions, judgments, and doubts of those who opposed Centering Prayer in its early years, and of those who may oppose it now, have been disproven by the positive results manifested in the lives, souls, and relationships of many thousands of long-time Centering Prayer practitioners. Here we have a large-scale field experiment that affirms the spiritual fruits and righteousness of Centering Prayer in the lives of those who practice it faithfully and appropriately. Bottom line: those who appropriately practice Centering Prayer become better Christians because the inner process of this prayer over time reduces and ultimately removes the obstacles in us to freely living the Gospel values in our daily life and relationships.

Centering Prayer has stirred up troubled waters for some "old wineskin" Christians who misunderstand it; and some of the people who oppose Centering Prayer, have, in turn, stirred up troubled waters for those of us who value and practice Centering Prayer. As Christians and reasonable human beings, we all need to recognize a magnanimous love, generosity, inclusiveness, and tolerance for one another under the Big Tent of our common Faith; and we need to practice the peace and love toward one another enjoined on us by Jesus.

What's always most important is not the outer form ("wineskin"), but the true inner Spirit (living "wine" of Christ); and in that living Holy Spirit we are all united in the Love of Christ. It is the divine passionate longing of our God, the Father in union with the Son and Holy

Spirit, "*to make known to us the riches of the glory of this mystery; that is Christ in you, the hope of glory,*" (adapted from Col. 1:27). It's through the long-term process of receiving the precious gift of silent contemplation (*however* we may access it), that we may enter into our eternal union with God and one another in the heart of Divine Love. With this in mind, let us say to all troubled waters, within and among us, as the resurrected Lord said to his frightened, disheartened disciples "*Peace, be with you,*" John 20:19. May the storms of fear and strife rest, and be calmed in the Lord's abiding peace within and among us.

8

DIVIDES AND THEIR CROSSING

Divides may be physical or nonphysical. Physical divides are crossed by building bridges between their two sides. Nonphysical divides are crossed by bringing their two sides together. Whatever brings the two sides of a nonphysical divide together is the bridge between them.

THE PRIMAL DIVIDE

The original or archetypal Divide in created reality is connected to the origins of God's Creation—which is happening within the Divine Consciousness. In order to create, the Consciousness of Divine Love—which is whole, complete, and perfect in itself—has entered into a state of limitation within itself to manifest something (created reality) that's less than itself. To do this, it's necessary to maintain the relatively real appearance of a separation or divide—actually multiple divides—within certain Spheres of the Divine Consciousness. This primal divide consists of two complementary poles or Universal Principles, with the basic undifferentiated energy of creation flowing back and forth in the space between them.[1] Creation's two opposite poles or Principles are the basic positive and negative charges, or Divine Masculine and Divine Feminine Principles. Their creative activity generates all the appearances, possibilities, and pairs of opposites in created reality (the visible and the invisible).

DIVIDING AND UNITING

Integration and evolution happen on all levels of creation via a repeating process of dividing and reuniting the energies of creation and consciousness. Opposites may attract or repel each other. They may complement (find completion in) each other, or they may conflict and negate each other. Hence, divides may be creative or destructive, positive or negative.

When Divine Perfection (God) creates, it has to enter into a condition of imperfection. The limitless enters into a state of limitation within itself, while yet remaining unlimited. There's a grand paradox or cosmic joke in this magical feat, as the Perfect plays at being imperfect, especially in us; and, from our side of the divine relationship, the many created appearances of limitation, separation, and imperfection are convincingly real to us, as human souls living our human condition.

So, the beginning and basis of Creation is dividing "the One" into "the Two" within "the One." This primal or archetypal divide is indicated in Genesis 1:27, "God created man in his image, in the divine image he created him; male and female he created them." The two sexes symbolize the positive and negative energies and poles that are present and active on all levels of created reality. Hence, division is the basic foundational principle of God's creative activity. All energy and consciousness (souls) in created reality experience the incompleteness of division and a deep inner longing to return to the completion and wholeness of non-created Reality. We all seek union with whom or what we feel may fulfill us. The integrating, uniting force of Divine Love, given us by God, offers the only true resolution and redemption of our incomplete "fallen [divided] condition."

THEOLOGICAL AND OTHER DIVIDES

The Western Model of "God-outside-the-soul and the-soul-outside-of-God" comes naturally from our initial self-conscious experiences of ourselves as human beings in the human condition. The Scriptural Model of "God-inside-the-soul and the-soul-inside-of-God" comes from the deeper discovery of our inner selves as spiritual beings. The stark difference between these two Models is the basis of the theological divide (as discussed in chapter 2). Each side of this divide has truth regarding the reality of human nature and existence. These two sides need to be brought together and integrated, to give us the full picture of whom and what we are. The natural attraction of complementary opposites expresses the soul's primal longing for completion and wholeness in the love of our Divine Source.

Divides exist and challenge us in all spheres of human life; in the inner and the outer, the social and the cultural, the economic and the religious, and so on. Perhaps the most critical divide of all is that existing in the soul between its human ground and its spiritual ground. This is the divide—from our side of the divine relationship—between the human being and God. We know ourselves primarily as human beings and not as spiritual beings. To become who we truly are, who God has created us to be, we need to get to know ourselves deeply as spiritual beings. This knowing—which is really loving and becoming, and in which LOVE is all that really matters—will ultimately and conclusively bridge the gaps of all that divides us from our self, God, one another, and from God's Creation.

DIVIDES AND SHADOW PLAY

Whenever we demonize a perceived opponent or enemy across a real or imaginary divide, we project our individual or group shadow (repressed unconscious contents) onto her, him, or them. This denies the other's precious reality as a fellow human and spiritual being. Such dehumanizing projections are evil acts of psychospiritual soul denial that reduce living, feeling individuals or groups of individuals down into a status of repulsive, despicable, subhuman objects—upon whom we may then project and act out our afflictive emotions against all that we hate, deny, and reject in ourselves. Such shadow projection is a basic component in the psychology of malicious war, bitter enmity, and the darker side of the divides that separate and alienate people from themselves and one another.

Shadow projection is the nefarious mechanism of psychological self-deception by which hatred, violence, and the abuse of others are so often motivated, rationalized, justified, and even glorified. This is truly "the work of Evil" that goes on in all types of negative polarizations where impassable divides exist within, among, and between individuals or groups. It's a primary obstacle to peace, understanding, and spiritual wellbeing in the soul and the world. When a negative polarization occurs, individuals either tend to shut down communications altogether; or else they "talk *at* each other" without really listening *to* each other. The unhappy results of such a "hardening of the heart" are usually loneliness, estrangement, enmity, and the unfeeling dehumanization of fellow human beings.

In the individual soul, we suffer the divide between our human ground and our spiritual ground, our false self and our true self, our outer role-playing persona and the feeling heart of our deep inner self. In human relations and the world, there are social, political, economic, religious, racial, ethnic, cultural, sexual, national, theological, and so many other divides. The cruel wars across these inner and outer divides, where the truth of the soul is denied, are like an angry cat or dog furiously chasing and biting at its own tail; the more it bites, the angrier it becomes. The only lasting resolution to this universal human dilemma—which is playing itself out on all levels of human life—will be a planetary spiritual awakening in which the Love of Christ is resurrected and perceived directly in all souls—as Tielhard de Chardin and others have proclaimed.[2] Before this healing of the negative divides can happen, we all need to withdraw our split-off toxic projections of shadowy unconscious contents from others, and, with God's help, we need to integrate them into consciousness and the truth of our soul—as is facilitated by the unloading of the unconscious. Only then shall Truth prevail and Love be revealed in and among us. Until humans come to consciously recognize that we are all one though many in the light, life, and love of our common spiritual ground, peace on Earth, goodwill to one another, and prosperity of soul in the collective will likely elude us.

SOME COMMONALITIES OF DIVIDES

One basic focus in this book is the theological divide separating two opposite approaches to our spiritual life and the divine relationship. We may gain a better understanding of the divides within Christianity by seeing how much the tragedies of these misunderstandings share in common with the dehumanizing alienations and unconscious projections present in all the negative, toxic divides that turn human beings against themselves and one another. Though the outer issues may differ widely, the inner pattern of all unhealthy divides within and among human souls remains the same. This inner pattern always involves a negation of our self and others as spiritual beings created in God's image and likeness. There's over-focusing on the human differences that divide us, and under-focusing on the deeper truth of the spiritual ground of love we all share in common as daughters and sons of God.

In the binary drama and game of our human adventure—where the opposites dance in creation's tragicomic play—it inevitably comes down to a clash of love versus hate—the archetypal conflict of Good versus Evil; or Love, Truth, and Freedom versus Hatred, Lies, and Slavery.[3] This drama is being played out in the life of each individual soul, and in the collective relations among all souls on Earth and beyond. When we demonize *anyone*, we contribute to the evil in the world, and we empower the evil in ourselves. This serves to perpetuate the divides that alienate us from Christ and our inner spiritual ground.

For this reason, as Christians, we are called to sincerely strive to overcome the divisions of all divides that separate and turn us against one another, especially when those divides are based on misunderstandings due to false, inaccurate, or incomplete information, e.g., the mistaken criticisms of Centering Prayer. As Jesus tells us, the world will know we are his disciples by our love for one another (John 13:35). Love partakes of the divine perspective and is not vindictive or blinded by any afflictive emotions. Love unites our divides and is yet always free to feel and express *all* emotions under appropriate circumstances. Love is not one-sided.

PRAYER AND DIVINE UNION

Our created human faculties (memory, intellect, emotions, imagination, and physical senses), wondrous as they are, cannot possibly contain or express the fullness of what God is, the fullness of Love, the Holy Mystery. Yet they may receive, contain, and express *kataphatic* radiations of God's presence. Our created human faculties are limited instruments—as is our evolving personality and consciousness that contains our faculties and derives its characteristics from *how* we choose to use them. To be honest and realistic, we need to humbly accept the fact that everything we have comes from God, the omnipresent, non-created Source, Sustainer, and Ground of created reality and our soul. Keeping this awareness in mind may allow us to view all reality from the root of true perspective within us—which is perfectly sane and non-delusional.

Recognizing the limitations of our given human faculties together with the human persona and identity that they express and support is by no means a rejection of those faculties or of our human self. This humble recognition is, rather, a first step toward positioning our self to realistically and most effectively relate to God from our side of the divine relationship. We may pray and relate to God through all of our faculties, including our physical body and senses; and we may experience partial radiations of the divine presence through all of our senses and faculties—especially our higher intuitive faculty, which is a spiritual faculty of the soul.

Most of the different ways of prayer and worship correlate to our senses and faculties; and all of these, by God's grace, may give us partial experiences of the divine manifesting to us in created reality. In fact, creation itself and its living symbolism contain multiple messages of intrinsic communication and wonder from God's Divine Consciousness to our limited evolving consciousness as human beings and spiritual beings. Such partial experiences of God always leave us longing for more because partial union with our soul's Divine Beloved—through our faculties and senses—ignites the soul's deep hunger and longing for full union with the Lord in the Love of Christ that is yet to come.

Precious communications from the Divine Mystery coming through our faculties and senses are progressive steps of spiritual courtship inviting our soul to journey further beyond our human faculties and senses into the Mystery Itself. The simple practical means for entering into the Mystery of non-created Reality—which bridges our inner spiritual divide and is beyond our faculties and senses—is what we in the Christian Contemplative Tradition call "*apophatic* contemplation" or "resting in God." Centering Prayer is one contemporary way of asking for this gift, and of preparing our faculties, especially our intuitive faculty, to receive it to whatever extent may be possible for us in this life. In his book, *Contemplative Prayer*, Thomas Merton makes a very important point concerning the gift of contemplation in prayer and action:

> We must approach our meditation realizing that "grace," "mercy," and "faith" are not permanent inalienable possessions which we gain by our efforts and retain as though by right, provided we behave ourselves. They are constantly renewed gifts. The life of grace in our hearts is renewed from moment to moment, directly and personally by God in his love for us. (p. 69)

This insightful teaching from Fr. Merton points to the living, ongoing dynamic of subtle back-and-forth communication between the soul and God in the divine relationship. There's nothing static about it in its ongoing spontaneity and creativity.

In *The Documents of Vatican II*, the "Decree on the Appropriate Renewal of the Religious Life" (*Perfectae Caritatis*) calls to all priests and religious, proclaiming, "As they seek God before all things and only Him, the members of each community *should combine contemplation with apostolic love.* By the former they adhere to God in mind and heart; by the latter they strive to associate themselves with the work of redemption and to spread the Kingdom of God" (p. 470).

The Method of Centering Prayer was created out of the preexisting Christian Contemplative Tradition in response to this Vatican II call for renewing the contemplative dimension of the Gospel. It was created by three Cistercian priests and monks, Frs. William Meninger, Basil Pennington, and Thomas Keating, men who, "seeking God before all things," dedicated their lives to the Gospel of Jesus, the Roman Catholic Church (and all Christians), to the lifelong study, practice, and teaching of Christian spirituality and its Contemplative Tradition, and "to the work of redemption and spreading the Kingdom of God."

Only in the gift of silent contemplation—where we do nothing and God does everything in us—may the soul journey gradually through its human ground into its spiritual ground to eventually experience and become the fullness of Divine Love in the Mystery of Christ. As Gail Fitzpatrick-Hopler, a founding member and president of Contemplative Outreach, has said, "The true self is inside the false self." This valuable insight tells us that our human ground and our spiritual ground are intimately connected. The false-self identity of our separate human persona and the true identity of our life in Christ are not really separated by a divide that we need to cross. It's our false self that perceives and maintains the divide. Our true spiritual identity is always present within us, like a diamond covered in mud. We simply need, with God's help in the gift of contemplation, to wash the mud off of our diamond. That is, we need to journey again and again over time in receptive contemplation from our outer surface self on the soul's changing periphery, through the secret shadows of its unconscious depths, to return home at last to our deep inner self in the soul's abiding true center. We do not make this inner journey alone because the Holy Spirit is here within us, to guide and protect us.

9

BRIDGING CREATED REALITY
TO NON-CREATED REALITY

Bridging created reality into non-created reality is the consummation of divine light and love in the life of the soul. It's the soul's great homecoming into God, following its epic journey through the vicissitudes and trials of created reality and human ground. Once we discover the reality of the divine relationship and choose to pursue this spiritual mystery of our soul in partnership with Christ, a dramatic shift of perspective and motivation begins subtly stirring within us, as we learn to transition from willful self-reliance to consenting and cooperating with God's presence and action in us and in our life. This is the movement from the stage of our necessary separate-self reliance into God-reliance and the deeper gift of silent *apophatic* prayer wherein the Holy Spirit brings us, step by step, through the inner transformation process and into the consummation of the divine relationship and our new life in Christ.

JOINING THE OPPOSITES

To originate and maintain created reality, God is manifesting a vast multidimensional energy field of limitations and incompleteness within the Divine Consciousness—which remains eternally whole, complete, unlimited, and perfect in its self as non-created reality. The infinite integrity of God's limitless light, eternal life, and divine love is the governing basis and evolutionary aim of God's Creation—as consciousness and individual souls evolve up through Nature's Kingdoms and human ground into our eternal spiritual ground. From the beginning, the Primal Divide, separating the positive and negative or masculine and feminine polarities, gives rise to the innumerable pairs of opposites proliferating throughout created reality within the Divine Consciousness. Hence, duality exists within nonduality, and the conceptual exists within the inconceivable (God).

On God's side of the divine relationship, the opposites are relative integrated manifestations within the nondual consciousness of Absolute Unity (Divine Love). In created reality, our side of the divine relationship, the opposites appear to be eternally separate absolutes, limiting and defining the phenomena of changing creation dancing back and forth between them in space and time, e.g., day and night, life and death, fear and trust, innocence and guilt, love and war, Good and Evil. Created reality—wherein we dwell—has come into existence out of non-created Reality *within* non-created Reality. So, from God's omni-perspective, there's never any separation or divide between the two (God and God's Creation), as there is from our many micro-perspectives within created reality. Divides exist only in created reality from our human side of the divine relationship. The movements of evolution and growth through human ground into spiritual ground require joining the opposites together—i.e., integrating the energies and bridging the divides within and among us. This is the Holy Spirit's creative work of love in the soul to which we're all called to consent.

JOINING THE TWO MODELS

God's union with us in love preexists from God's side of the divine relationship. The mysterious Divine Consciousness is inclusive of *all* created reality. Hence, we may call it "nondual" or "undivided." The Scriptural Model of "God-in-the-soul and the-soul-in-God" points directly to the nondual or mystical intuition of God and our divine relationship, which integrates the soul in God, dawning in consciousness as a progressively unfolding natural complement to the initial dualistic perspectives of the Primal Divide and the Western Model, where God is assumed to be absolutely separate and outside the soul.

The Western Model of God and that of our relationship to God originates from our side of the divine relationship in stages of human consciousness where there is as yet no direct awareness of our preexisting intimate union with God. Hence, the Western Model is based in the binary logic of dualistic thinking and, in its extremes, assumes the divide separating human souls from God to be permanent and absolute. This early model inadvertently imposes limitations on God and often tends to envision God in terms of *kataphatic* images that are unconscious mirror projections of deified human attitudes, ideals, and characteristics. Hence, it's inevitably a model of limited concrete thinking, bound to the pairs of opposites, and incomplete in its vision of the Ultimate Reality. The anthropomorphic Western Model, in all its variations, precedes finer abstract thinking and belongs to earlier stages of human development and evolving consciousness. This explains why there are sometimes stark contradictions between the distant, wrathful God of the Old Testament, and the loving, merciful, and intimate Father God (*Abba*) introduced by Jesus in the New Testament.

Growing through the Western Model is a necessary process of development for all of us, and it's legitimate to remain in it as long as we need to; until we're ready and wanting to expand and deepen our ideas of God and our participation in the divine relationship. Spiritual growth within the Western Model involves a movement from one extreme side of the theological divide toward its center, and toward acknowledging that it is indeed possible for God to become present and active in the soul. Traditionalist Christian contemplatives and other devout souls in the Western Model, particularly those inclined toward the teachings of venerable Christian mystics like John of the Cross and Teresa of Avila (see below), embrace the idea that the Lord may and will become present and active in us only when we sincerely desire this and *if* we're "in a state of grace." They assume that God cannot and will not enter into the soul as long as it's not in a state of grace; because God is pure, undefiled, and will not enter into a soul that is tainted by serious sin and by the presence of Evil.

In this pious belief regarding purity and being in "a state of grace," the Western Model may be placing limitations on God (when actually the limitations are with us); but it is also taking decisive steps across the theological divide in the direction of the Scriptural Model. The Scriptural Model, as we're presenting it here, assumes that the divine indwelling is always present—at least as latent potential—in the soul, whether the soul is primarily in a state of sin or grace. Here we have a clear division of opinions based on the root assumptions of the two models. If we look to the Scriptures or to the *Catholic Catechism*, we may find passages supporting both points of view.

As Thomas Keating has pointed out, when Jesus, in the Garden of Gethsemane, asked the Father, "*if it is possible, let this cup pass from me*" (Matt. 26:39), drinking the cup of identification with all human suffering, sin, and alienation from God meant that he would lose the grace of his conscious personal connection of intimacy and union with the Father in the divine relationship.[1] This would seem to affirm the Western-model mystic's view that the consequence of not being in a state of grace is the conscious experience of separation from God. It does not, however, negate the idea that, from God's side of the divine relationship, God may still be secretly in union with the soul in the hidden depths of its unconscious. On the other hand, in Matthew 19:26, Jesus tells us "for God all things are possible." This essentially seems to tell us that for God there are no limitations because God is eternally free, infinite, and unbound by any of our humanly conceived ideas, projections, or expectations. All we know is that "God is love" (1 John 4:8, 16). The implications of this incredibly simple yet profound statement are most wonderful and boundless, if we take it as an absolute.

With this in mind, I feel it's pointless to argue over which theological model may be right and which may be wrong because, depending on our viewpoint, it's possible to see each of the two models as either right or wrong; and, in the kaleidoscope of partial perspectives conceivable in the human mind, it's possible to see both as right to a certain degree and as wrong to a certain degree. Since both, in their mystical or contemplative approaches, do agree that it's possible for the Holy Spirit to become present and active in the soul, so as to bring the soul into union with God in the Love of Christ, *this* is their point of meeting and joining together across the divide in the Love of Christ. To the degree that this ideal becomes a reality in the soul, disagreements and arguments between the two models and their theological assumptions become irrelevant, childish, and meaningless. God will work with us regardless of which model or combination of models we identify with. The point of true relevance here is to be brought, by God's grace, into divine union because, ultimately, *Love is all that matters*, not which partial perspective or opinion is right and which is wrong.

THE SOUL'S HOMECOMING

The Western Model tends to glorify and project onto God the limitations of ego that are characteristic of human beings. In so doing, we create God (our ideas of God) in our image and likeness. This is actually a form of unconscious idolatry. Ego originates from division (the Primal Divide), and is born of self-reflecting consciousness beholding its own reflection in the mirror of duality. When this is our basis of reality in human ground, then our images of God will also become dualistic reflections in that self-same mirror. Hence, we have the Western Model of "God-outside-the-soul and the-soul-outside-of-God." This is the God of our limited understanding and invention, a stepping stone toward God's Reality that's yet to be revealed. Our ideas and images of God are not the true unknown God of non-created Reality's eternally inconceivable Mystery—i.e., the Triune God of intimate relationships in unlimited Divine Love.

The ego-self in human ground feels itself to be alone and incomplete. Its consciousness is a partial light of living experience longing and looking for completion and wholeness. Thus, in human ground, we seek companionship in community, intimate personal relationships, and in society where groups of partial human lights may come together in relationships to create greater lights in which, ideally, each may find itself reflected inside the other or others. If, by God's grace, we add the Love of Christ into this mixture of interacting human lights and energy fields, then we'll have the transformation of our separate-self human consciousness into the nondual unified field of divine consciousness, the revelation of our true self, and our soul's graced participation in God's holy spiritual ground.

The power of Divine Love generates an integrating–transforming consciousness inside created reality and in the life of the soul. Love is the ultimate nonduality that draws everything together so that, ultimately, there shall be no absolute divides of separation within or among the hearts and minds of individual souls. Divine Love is the soul force of Christ that completes God's creation by bridging created reality and all the souls in it into non-created Reality. This is our spiritual homecoming that completes the circle of creation within us.

THREE TYPES OF CONSCIOUSNESS[2]

The bridge bringing created reality into non-created Reality, or duality into nonduality, is formed by three types of evolving consciousness that emerge out of a primal monistic energy field and consciousness of undifferentiated unity. This primal consciousness is the original energy circulating across the Primal Divide between the positive and negative poles at the beginning of creation. It is the undifferentiated blissful energy of life's pure springing fountains out of which all forms and living beings in creation are eventually fashioned.[3]

The experience of a developing fetus in its mother's womb is said to be an expression of this undifferentiated primal unity in synergy with the mother. This experience becomes a primal memory in the human soul which, in its incomplete divided state, the soul unconsciously longs to return to by way of regression; that is, by going back to its beginnings as opposed to evolving forward through the human condition and into its spiritual ground, as intended by God.

The impetus to return into the undifferentiated peace and bliss of primal monistic unity in life's pure springing fountains is a powerful instinctual force in human nature and sexuality. When taken too far, and in the absence of love, it leads to overindulgences and becomes a blind quest for self-transcendence leading us into various unhealthy addictions that block and oppose the soul's higher longing for human and spiritual growth.

The three types of evolving consciousness that grow out of our original monistic consciousness in the womb are: 1) the separating consciousness of duality; 2) the connecting consciousness of relationships; and 3) the integrating, transforming consciousness of nonduality. These three may form a bridge across the divide separating created reality from non-created reality in consciousness on our side of the divine relationship.

The binary separating consciousness is generated by our experiences of contrasts, the pairs of opposites, and our tendencies to approach or avoid what we experience—e.g., pleasure or pain. Experiences of interest/attraction or pain/revulsion tend to focus and amplify the separating consciousness, wherein we learn to distinguish between "me" and "not me." Our separate-self sense of ego identity arises within the separating consciousness. Without this consciousness, we'd be unable to function or survive in human ground. In relation to God and our experience of existential aloneness/incompleteness, the separating consciousness is the genesis of the Western Model.

The connecting consciousness grows out of the objective separating consciousness when we feel attraction to another combined with a tendency to relate and co-identify to some degree on a subjective feeling level. The basis for the connecting consciousness is established in early life when an infant bonds with its mother. This bonding creates the "blueprint" for the connecting consciousness in all our subsequent relationships. If the separating consciousness is the starting point for relationships on the acquaintanceship level, then the connecting consciousness, as it deepens, is the basis for relationships on the friendliness and friendship levels. The separating consciousness is always present in the connecting consciousness, but it gets reduced or relativized within the larger context of the connecting consciousness, where we feel less separate or detached from the other, and we become less self-centered. This applies to our relationships with other people as well as to the divine relationship.

The integrating, transforming consciousness correlates to the "full intimacy or union of life" level of relationship. This mysterious consciousness equates to Christ or the Holy Spirit and is the hidden vehicle of the divine action in our soul. It is nondual (without an opposite or equal) and includes the other types of consciousness within itself. Divine Love is the active motivating force of the integrating, transforming consciousness—which brings together (integrates) all the disparate energies and opposites in the soul, in order to heal and transform us in Christ. We experience little flashes and intimations of the integrating, transforming consciousness whenever things "come together" for us, whenever we feel "at one" with anyone or anything, and whenever we feel whole and complete.

Every experience of authentic love is an experience of God and of the nondual integrating, transforming consciousness—which creates instant intimacy and unites all in its sphere of activity while preserving the individuality, uniqueness, and integrity of everything that it integrates. In our prayer life, the integrating, transforming consciousness corresponds to the gift of *apophatic* contemplation into which Centering Prayer leads us. This nondual consciousness integrates its contents into a harmonious unity while preserving their individual characteristics. Thus, it preserves the primal monistic, separating, and connecting consciousnesses within itself on higher levels of unity and wholeness. In so doing, the integrating, transforming consciousness bridges created reality into non-created Reality, bringing all that precedes it into God. The nondual oneness of this integrating, transforming consciousness may not be conceived by the intellect. It is nonlinear, paradoxical, and may be sensed or received only intuitively, like the gift of *apophatic* contemplation.

≈

The following, simple diagram tries to objectify some of the above ideas. The headings in bold italics divide the diagram into four vertical columns; in terms of the three main types of consciousness, their corresponding perspectives, and where we experience them (Locus and Realm of Reality). The separating consciousness is objective and thinking based. The connecting consciousness is subjective and feeling based. These first two correspond to created reality and are the types of consciousness with which we are most familiar as human beings. The deeper nondual integrating, transforming consciousness is a mystery to us.

This third type of consciousness is in a class by itself, since it includes and transcends created reality; and its true center (which appears as a tiny point at the bottom of the "V" in the diagram) is actually everywhere (cf. St. Augustine, "God is a circle whose center in everywhere and whose circumference is nowhere"). Hence, the integrating, transforming consciousness and its omnipresent true center correspond to God or non-created Reality. It is the hidden, nondual container, origin, and sustainer of everything in created reality. The first two types of consciousness (separating and connecting) may be experienced separately or together. The nondual integrating, transforming consciousness in its fullness includes *all* types of consciousness and thus has no equal or opposite—just as God as Divine Consciousness has no equal or opposite. Hence, the bottom section of the diagram—that of the nondual integrating, transforming consciousness)—actually contains the two sections above it (those of the separating and connecting consciousnesses), as well as existing eternally in its own Reality of divine love, truth, and freedom beyond creation.

In relating to God from the limited perspectives of the separating consciousness or the connecting consciousness, we may imagine that God has an opposite, but this is only our limited thinking. It's not a true or accurate reflection of God as God actually is, nothing we're capable of thinking or imagining could possibly be. We may relate to God from any perspective or type of consciousness indicated on the below diagram. These differing perspectives and types of consciousness are what give rise to differing theologies (e.g., Monism, Theism, Pantheism, and Panentheism), and to the theological divide between the Western and Scriptural Models. Just as the nonconceptual may not be expressed in concepts, our ideas of God are not God. At best, they are pointers to God's Ultimate Mystery. With this in mind, we may now study the following, humble diagram.

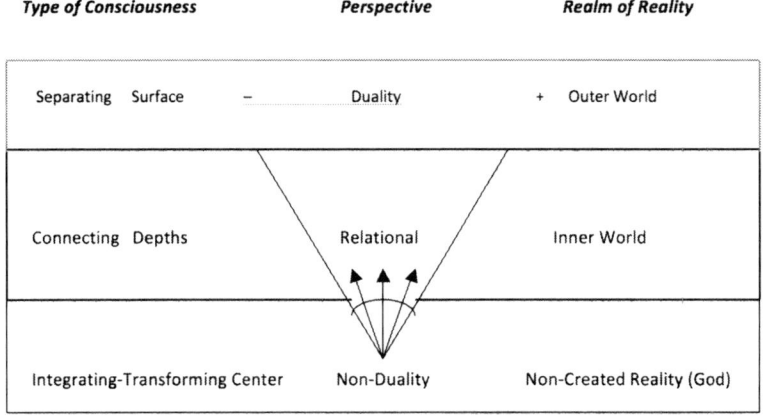

Type of Consciousness	*Perspective*	*Realm of Reality*
Separating Surface –	Duality +	Outer World
Connecting Depths	Relational	Inner World
Integrating-Transforming Center	Non-Duality	Non-Created Reality (God)

WHAT IS NONDUALITY?

Nonduality is a mystery toward which words, concepts, and images may, at best, point. We all know what duality is because this is a basic parameter of our separating consciousness and experience in created reality and human ground, derived from the Primal Divide. Duality structures much of our daily-life experience and is all about differences, divides, distances, and the objectivity of what's "out there." So how are we to cross the bridge from duality to nonduality separating created reality from non-created Reality and the soul from God (on our side of the divine relationship)? Since the nondual Divine is beyond concepts, we'll close this discussion by mentioning some concrete spiritual images and ideas that may point our intuitive intellect and creative imagination toward God's Holy Mystery.

1. Jesus' analogy of "the vine and the branches" in John 15:4–5 is a wonderful vital image pointing to this Mystery and to the intimacy of the divine relationship: "Remain in me, as I remain in you. Just as a branch cannot bear fruit unless it remains on the vine, so neither can you unless you remain in me. I am the vine, you are the branches. Whoever remains in me and I in him [or her] will bear much fruit, because without me you can do nothing." The "vine" is One and its "branches" are many. Each branch, like each human soul, draws its life from the One Vine. Each branch is unique and individual; yet all belong to the same vine that gives them life. This is a profound metaphor for nonduality and the integrating, transforming consciousness, "old wine" in a "new wineskin."

The branches are all distinct from one another but not really separate in the deeper level of the vine (spiritual ground) that unites them. Each branch (soul) that remains spiritually in the love of Christ bears good fruit. Apart from the eternal values of the Gospel, and without the inner nourishment of the divine indwelling, none of us can do anything of enduring spiritual value in human life. The vine-and-branches analogy illustrates perfectly the relationship between the individual soul's separate-self persona (false self) and the divine indwelling of Christ, the one true vine of Father, Son, and Holy Spirit in the true center of our being. Christ is the spiritual vine and center of Divine Love uniting us all in the nondual ground of our Source.

2. The nonbinary Mystery of the integrating, transforming consciousness (which includes the Western Model), and our oneness in Christ is further indicated in Jesus' moving prayer to the Father in John 17:20–26:

> I ask not only on behalf of these, but also on behalf of those who will believe in me through their word, that they may all be one. As you, Father, are in me and I am in you, may they also be in us.... The glory that you have given me I have given them, so that they may be one as we are one, I in them and you in me, that they may become completely one...Righteous Father.... I made your name known to them, and I will make it known, so

that the love with which you have loved me may be in them, and
I in them.

These beautiful words of Jesus' prayer reveal the nondual intimacy of
the divine relationship into which we're all invited—and wherein we
already are on God's side of the relationship.

3. Duality and nonduality are integrated and united in the Mystery
of the Holy Trinity. The idea of "One God in Three Persons"—Father,
Son, and Holy Spirit—expresses the nondual paradox of dynamic loving relationship in the unity of Divine Love's living oneness, i.e., God
as Three-in-One and One-in-Three. We may see the three types of consciousness present and active in the Mystery of the Trinity: 1) the separating consciousness identifies each of the Three Divine Persons as an
individual component that is present and active within the One; 2) the
connecting consciousness is present and active in the continuing loving
flow of interrelationships in the Trinity; and 3) the integrating, transforming consciousness is present and active as the oneness that unites
them in the boundless creativity through which God is continually manifesting all that is or may be. This is not a static monistic God outside
of or limited to created reality; but a fathomless dynamic Mystery of
eternal Love, Truth, and Freedom simultaneously embracing and transcending "the visible and the invisible" without limit. This Mystery is
not reducible to the logic of rational thought (as in the Western Model),
but its subtle presence may, by God's grace, be intuitively intimated
or sensed via the gift of *apophatic* contemplation, and in moments of
spontaneous spiritual insight—as in unexpected experiences of love
and compassion inspiring and enlightening our consciousness.

BRIDAL MYSTICISM

"As a young man marries a virgin, your Builder shall marry you;
and as a bridegroom rejoices in his bride, so shall your God rejoice
in you" (Isa. 62:5). Our soul's "builder" is Christ, the Word of the
Father (John 1:1–7). Allegorically, the bride's virginity symbolizes

the purity of heart in which our soul's lost innocence is restored in
God's love, to complement the wisdom gained through our experiences of duality in human life. In Christian Bridal Mysticism, which
is also inspired by the Old Testament's "Song of Songs," the soul
becomes the "bride of Christ" in the spiritual journey's culmination
through the inner birthing process of contemplative prayer carried
on within us by the Holy Spirit, as we freely consent and cooperate with this grace. This holy process, which involves the soul's
complete purification, healing, illumination, and transformation,
carries us across the bridge linking created reality to non-created
Reality: that is, it's the soul's integration fully into God from our
side of the divine relationship.

As humans are made in God's *"image and likeness, male and
female"* (Gen. 1:26–27), the joining of the sexes symbolizes the union
of opposites in the soul while their separation represents the Primal
Divide at the beginning of creation. All genuine love is integrating,
transforming, and nondual. Divine Love is the ultimate nonduality.
The principle of duality expresses the Primal Divide and is mirrored in
how we humans are physically created as male and female. The living
symbolism present in creation contains ongoing messages of mystery
to us from our Holy Creator.

The separation of male and female energies in created reality is duality (the separating consciousness). The mutual attractions and arousal
of the sexes is the bridge of connecting consciousness between them
(duality seeking unity through relationship); and their climatic exchang-
ing and merging energies together to become "one flesh" (Gen. 2:24)
in loving communion and union represents the fulfillment stage of the
integrating, transforming consciousness—i.e., bridal mysticism and the
ideal sacrament of marriage. This delightful wonder is God's creation
and life-affirming gift to us. Ultimately, the integration of duality into
nonduality is the bridging of created reality into God (Divine Love).

The consummation of Bridal Mysticism in Love's nondual oneness may be intimated allegorically in intuitions of two imaginary
lovers exploring, discovering, and celebrating the shining holy

mystery of God's presence in one another: They're not only one and they're not just two in this loving communion and union; they're both one and two and more in the timeless transcendent moments of their wondrous joining together. It's the sudden glimpsing of God in another that causes us to fall and rise in love, as we're briefly transported from time into eternity. All experiences of love are experiences of God. We can't imagine or reduce to thought *what* this elusive love actually is. Love transcends the objective intellect, creating instant subjective intimacy. It's something, however fleeting or lasting, that's suddenly revelatory, transcendent, and divine. As the anonymous *Cloud of Unknowing* tells us, "What the mind cannot grasp, the heart may embrace." This is a most profound contemplative insight.

The spirit of Bridal Mysticism is expressed profoundly and beautifully in the simplicity of *The Dark Night of the Soul*, the well-known poem by John of the Cross: "Oh night that was my guide/oh night more loving than the morning sun/Oh night that joined the lover/to the beloved/transforming each of them into the other."[4] Such is the divine romance of God and the soul.

The image of a heavenly wedding, as well as of a royal banquet, appears in the Scriptures to allegorically represent the soul's joyous homecoming and inner union with God. Those purified souls who "have washed their robes and made them white in the blood of the Lamb" (Rev. 7:14), are the ones who may enter the bridal chamber within the soul to consummate their union with Christ in the innocence, purity, and love of the divine relationship. This is the soul's final rebirth into the heavenly kingdom of spiritual ground within us—where nothing may deprive us of our divine inheritance.

The *Catholic Catechism* (p. 268, par. 1,027) speaks of the soul's communion and union with God as follows: "This mystery of blessed communion with God and all who are in Christ is beyond all understanding and description [i.e., it's apophatic]. Scripture speaks of it in images: life, light, peace, wedding feast, wine of the kingdom, the Father's house, the heavenly Jerusalem, paradise: 'no eye has seen, nor ear heard, nor the heart of man conceived, what God has prepared for those who love him'" (1 Cor. 1:9).

≈

To present a concrete historical example of advanced contemplative spirituality and Christian Bridal Mysticism, let's look at some brief excerpts from Teresa of Avila's classic work, *The Interior Castle* (1577), where she writes of the "mystical marriage" and the stages of the spiritual journey as she personally experienced them. As Raimundo Panikkar mentions in his Preface to *The Interior Castle*, we can't do justice in a brief summary to the spiritual climate and historical context in which *The Interior Castle* was written; and certainly this also applies to the detailed and nuanced contents of the book. So what we're doing here is simply to point to it as the excellent and inspiring example of Bridal Mysticism that it is.

Teresa's unique experiences of the spiritual journey involved a most unusual "lights on" mysticism; that is, they involved a path of contemplative mysticism in which various highly extraordinary spiritual phenomena or "favors from the Lord" occurred. In describing "The Sixth Dwelling Place"[5] (the stage of "Spiritual Espousal"), Teresa writes of a spiritual wound given by the Lord that the soul both suffers and enjoys: "It [the soul] complains to its Spouse with words of love... It knows He is present, but He doesn't want to reveal the manner in which He allows Himself to be enjoyed. And the pain is great, although delightful and sweet. And even if the soul does not want this wound, the wound cannot be avoided... The wound satisfies it much more than the delightful and painless absorption of the prayer of quiet" (p. 116). Teresa was brought into the Sixth Dwelling of her "lights on" map of the spiritual journey *after* abiding in the silent *apophatic* depths of the "prayer of quiet" in the "Fifth Dwelling Place."

Here, Teresa is writing about a subjective mystery and grace of the Lord's presence and action in the soul that comes (for those experiencing "lights on" Bridal Mysticism) *after* one has received the gifts of "infused recollection" and "the prayer of quiet," for which Centering Prayer serves to prepare us. The Carmelite Saint mentions how wordless communications from the soul's Spouse, who abides in the Seventh Dwelling Place, may cause the soul's human faculties (which are active in the first three dwelling places) to become perfectly still; and then, addressing the Lord, she proclaims: "O my powerful God, how sublime are your secrets, and how different spiritual things are from all that is visible and understandable here below" (p. 116). Teresa is a pioneering spiritual explorer, scout, and guide for us, mapping out the mysterious unknown territory of spiritual ground that awaits us as we journey deeper within and across the bridge from human ground and created reality into God as may be experienced from our human side of the divine relationship.

Teresa goes on to describe an inner warmth or "fire" of Divine Love that arises in the soul. This sacred fire of Divine Love burns hot and bright up to the limit of the soul's capacity to withstand it. Once that limit is reached, the fire goes out so that no damage is done to the soul. As the soul evolves and becomes increasingly purified, its capacity to withstand the inner fire of Divine Love also increases. Teresa writes regarding this incredible experience of intense intimacy in the divine relationship:

> This delightful pain—and it is not pain—is not continuous.... It is not something that can be procured in any human way ... It comes and goes [and] is never permanent. For this reason it doesn't set the soul on fire; but just as the fire is about to start, the spark goes out and the soul is left with the desire to suffer again that loving pain the spark causes.... The activity is not like that found in other feelings of devotion, where the great absorption in delight can make us doubtful. Here all the senses and faculties remain free of any absorption, wondering what this could be, without hindering anything or being able, in my opinion, to increase or take away that delightful pain. (*The Interior Castle*, p. 117)

In more recent times, some contemplatives have commented that God's Bridal Mysticism can, at times, awaken an amazing and delightful erotic component or quality in the soul. In all of this, we accept in good faith that the Lord will give us or not give us *whatever* we need to heal, grow spiritually, and what is appropriate for us at the present time in the divine relationship.

Writing of "The Seventh Dwelling Places," Teresa tells us:

> When His Majesty is pleased to grant the soul this divine marriage, He first brings it into His own dwelling place.... He gives the soul raptures.... In rapture He unites it with Himself.... When He joins it to Himself, it doesn't understand anything; for all the faculties are lost... When the soul is brought into that [seventh] dwelling place, the Most Blessed Trinity, all Three persons,...is revealed through a certain representation of the truth.... All three Persons communicate themselves to it...explaining those words of the Lord in the Gospel: that He and the Father and the Holy Spirit will come to dwell with the soul that loves Him and keeps his Commandments." (ibid., pp. 174–175)

The "lights on" experiences of "spiritual betrothal" that Teresa describes so well (in as much as this is possible) are not the normal experience of most Christian contemplatives (at least in our day), who occasionally may have "lights on" experiences but who are mostly in the "lights off" mode. As Thomas Keating points out in his original "Spiritual Journey" audio/video series (talks 18 and 19), the distinction between "lights on" and "lights off" mysticism is very important to understand; a key point being that *both* ways ultimately bring us, by God's grace, into the same mystical marriage and divine union. In Centering and Contemplative Prayer, how we subjectively experience the spiritual journey is up to God, not us. Which mode or combination of "lights on" and "lights off" is best for us, only God knows; so we entrust our self to the Lord, our "Maker" and divine therapist. The "lights off" path of Christian Contemplation and Bridal Mysticism is modeled for us in the writings of Teresa's beloved contemporary, collaborator, and spiritual director, John of the Cross (1542–1591), who, with Teresa (1515–1582), founded the reformed contemplative order of Discalced Carmelites.

John of the Cross' allegorical images and descriptions in his poem *The Dark Night of the Soul* in *The Ascent of Mount Carmel,* and in *The Dark Night,* plus his *Spiritual Canticle* and *Living Flame of Love,* are powerful and concise expressions of the spirituality of Christian Bridal Mysticism. The spiritual writings of John of the Cross take us through the entire spiritual journey, from human ground in "the Night of Sense," into spiritual ground in "the Night of Spirit," and beyond into the fullness of Divine Union in the Love of Christ. John of the Cross' "lights off" map of the spiritual journey, which overlaps significantly with Teresa of Avila's "lights on" map, includes what Thomas Keating, using modern language and pouring *old wine* and *new wine* into *new wineskins,* has described as "unloading the unconscious" and "the Divine Therapy."

Quoting John of the Cross in his illuminating preface to *The Interior Castle,* Raimundo Panikkar writes,

> "God has spoken One Word which is His Son and He has spoken it in eternal silence," says John of the Cross, repeating a common statement of the Fathers of the Church. In order to be incorporated into Him we must enter into that Silence, not only reducing to stillness all voices, images and thoughts about everything and even about God Himself, but reducing our very being into an ontological silence. "In order to have the All you must leave the All," including ourselves. (p. xvii)

John of the Cross cautions against "hankering after" the extraordinary phenomena of "lights on" experiences, as does Teresa. Attachment to such desires may easily become distractions and obstacles reinforcing the human ego or false self on the spiritual level. Thomas Keating once told me that if we're truly detached from desire for "spiritual experiences," that's when God is liable to give us more of them. If we get greedy for God's wonderful gifts and focus less on the Giver and more on the gifts, that's when God is more likely to take them away. This is part of how the Holy Spirit communicates and instructs us in the divine relationship.

Though we may certainly learn, benefit, and be inspired by study-ing the works of spiritual masters, it may not be helpful to expect or try to duplicate the spiritual experiences of people who lived in former times. Though God's basic Spiritual Laws and Principles are timeless, the *kataphatic* contents and means of their manifestations in our con-temporary souls and lives are liable to change with the contents and consciousness of the world in which we live. It's important to recall that God works in each of us individually and personally in a unique way, as God did with Teresa of Avila and John of the Cross. The Holy Spirit delights in doing "something new," in pouring its timeless sacred "*wine*" into "*new wineskins.*" We need to be open to this.

THREE STEPS ACROSS

At Contemplative Outreach's 2008 Annual Meeting in Pittsburg, Pennsylvania, Thomas Keating introduced a succinct summary of the divine relationship and spiritual journey that a monk at Saint Bene-dict's Monastery in Snowmass, Colorado had recently received in a dream. There are three basic steps or stages in this summary that take the soul across the divide between human ground and spiritual ground, and between created reality and non-created Reality. These three steps across the divide form a spiritual bridge linking the three types of consciousness mentioned above; that is, the binary separating consciousness, the relational connecting consciousness, and the non-dual and unifying integrating, transforming consciousness.

The first step comes at the beginning of the spiritual journey, when we realize that there really is a Higher Power or Divine Other (God). With God now part of our reality, this realization calls for some adjustments in our outlook and way of life; and we begin to live our life in relation to God to some degree, though perhaps from a respectable distance. We will likely adopt some perspectives of the Western Model in this first stage. Depending on our priorities in life, we may choose to remain in this initial stage of the spiritual jour-ney; or we may feel called to go deeper into the divine relationship, moving through the levels of friendliness into the more fully engaged and committed levels of friendship. It's always a free choice for us.

The second step involves responding to our soul's inner desire for a deeper, more intimate relationship with God. Here we discover the Scriptural Model and want to spend increasing amounts of time consciously relating to God via a variety of spiritual practices, e.g., prayer, worship, study, meditation, and service. In this second step, the divine relationship becomes an increasingly higher priority for us. As God responds to our inner longing, a new spiritual hunger awakens in our soul as we begin relating to God as our Divine Beloved. In this second step, we move out of the objective separating consciousness into the more emotionally caring connecting consciousness in relation to our God. Now, as love stirs in our soul, we want to become *one* with the Beloved Other. This desire is the main characteristic of the second step, and is the beginning of Bridal Mysticism in our spiritual life. At this point, we actively pursue the deepening of our connection to God in the divine relationship through various *kataphatic* and, possibly, *apophatic* religious practices, such as *Lectio Divina* and Centering Prayer.

It's the relational connecting consciousness of this second step that begins moving us across the bridge between created reality and non-created Reality. Our longing for God and our humble consenting to the divine action in our soul activate the integrating, transforming consciousness of Christ and the Holy Spirit within us. The secret activity of the integrating, transforming consciousness gradually clears away the obstacles to Divine Union in us, so we may indeed become the spiritual bride of Christ. As this wonderful consummation gradually comes about, by virtue of the divine action in us and our willing consent and deepening cooperation in contemplative prayer, we begin to enter the third step of our spiritual journey into God on the far side of the bridge. In this third step or stage, "*We realize that there is no Other,*" because we discover that, in the all-inclusive, all-embracing Divine Perspective in which we now share, everything is in God and God is in all things.

This revolutionary realization may not be accurately imagined or grasped from the limited perspectives of the separating and connecting consciousness. Its unending revelation of eternal Divine Love is utterly *apophatic* and inconceivable to the intellect. This third and climatic step into Divine Union does not negate our soul's unique individuality, as some critics mistakenly assume. On the contrary, Divine Union in the Love of Christ completes and fulfills our soul's individuality as nothing else can. As Paul tells us in 1 Corinthians 12:27: "Now all of you together are Christ's body, and each one of you is a separate and necessary part of it." The fullness of Divine Union is the completion stage of the integrating–transforming consciousness that bridges and brings created reality into non-created Reality; that is, everything in created reality (including the separating and connecting consciousness) is brought along and lovingly integrated into the macro-perspective of the Divine Consciousness.

Love is the supreme Law of mercy and forgiveness that carries us across the bridge of separation from the Lord into our divine inheritance as sons and daughters of God. This inner crossing is our soul's epic journey from isolation in the separating consciousness, through growing relatedness and co-identity in the connecting consciousness, and finally into the fullness of the nondual integrating, transforming consciousness in Christ. In light of this perspective, it seems an instructive irony that holy love—which we need so much to be whole and complete, and which is so often experienced as elusive, fleeting, and tenuous in human ground—should also be the eternal wellspring and foundation of created reality and God's spiritual ground. Precious Love, which seems most temporary and possibly unreal in time-bound human ground, is actually what's most real and permanent in our soul's timeless spiritual ground—where we've originally come from.

Relating to God as "Other," especially as the Beloved Other, is an essential part of being human in the divine relationship. We never outgrow this as long as we're a human self. At the same time, we're not meant to remain limited to feeling separate from God either. In the fullness of our love for God and life, we're free to relate to our Divine

Source through all three types of evolving consciousness (separating, connecting, and integrating–transforming); and in terms of the three basic steps or stages of recognition, longing, and union with the Holy Other. The fullness of this is what the integrating, transforming consciousness actually is, at least while we're living in and identified with our human ground. When we leave this life, we shall no longer be limited human beings. The fullness of what we shall become in God and the Love of Christ is yet to be revealed.

≈

Humbly and gratefully accepting our human self as we truly are is an act of love and wisdom needing fresh renewal each day of our life. Each of us is a tiny light of God's presence. When we put two or more of these tiny lights together, we make a bigger light to share in together. When our combined lights are graced by God's presence and action, God's presence grows in all of us and we are blessed. Hence, we may all share together in the divine relationship.

The gift of contemplation—for which Centering Prayer prepares us—is the practical means for God to bring us closer and closer into full intimacy. We may access this gift in any number of ways, as God chooses to offer it. We need the *kataphatic* forms of devotion, worship, and study to relate to God and bring us across the great divide (from our human side) separating created reality from non-created Reality. The *kataphatic* forms of meditation, prayer, and religion begin in the initial stages of the separating consciousness (where God is perceived as "Other"). They continue further, taking us across the bridge of the connecting consciousness (where we long to grow closer and become one with the Beloved Other); and, as God responds from God's side of the divine relationship, we're gradually brought, via the secret gift of silent, receptive contemplation, into the unifying, nondual heart of Christ's integrating, transforming consciousness beyond and within created reality into the *apophatic* love, truth, and freedom of the Divine Consciousness where *"God is all in all"* and *"there is no 'Other.'"*

APPENDIX: SILENCE AND SOLITUDE

I

A silent retreat is an opportunity to slow down and pause into the simplicity of the present moment, which is always God's present moment. It is an opportunity to deepen our awareness and participation in the immediacy of what is right now as we attend to the simplicity of whatever is before us. Thomas Keating writes in his book, *Intimacy With God*:

> St. John of the Cross wrote, "The Father spoke one word from all eternity and he spoke it in silence, and it is in silence that we hear it" (p. 15). This suggests that silence is God's first language and that all other languages are poor translations. The discipline of Centering Prayer and the other traditional practices are ways of refining our receptive apparatus so that we can perceive the word of God communicating itself with ever greater simplicity to our spirit and our inmost being.

The inner silence of the present moment is as timeless and unfathomable as the depths of the divine. Everyone's individual being is rooted in these divine depths, the holy ground of God's eternal presence within and among us. In the simplicity of interior silence and personal solitude we may commune with these depths as they speak to us in the language of pure presence.

God is not a future being or a past being but always the deepest and most present now-being of this open, living moment. Our solitude is the personal existential aloneness and privacy of our individual being in our self and in relation to God. Let us support each other in sacred solitude on this retreat as we journey together into a communion of silence before God in the wordless simplicity of each present moment.

| |

As we enter the silence of these days in retreat, we are leaving aside our normal preoccupations with linear worldly time and space, opening our self to discover and engage time's sacred dimension that is always in the present moment, in the timeless depths of silence. This sacred space where eternity intersects time is always with us, always present to us as the timeless dimension of the open now-moment. It is the sacred space of prayer, ritual, and communion with our God.

In deliberately entering into silence on this retreat, we are seeking to become increasingly present to our self as we are and to the divine presence within and among us. To foster and support our depth of silent communion with the Lord, let us become what poet Rainer Maria Rilke called "guardians of each other's solitude." Solitude is the place of deep inner communion with self and God, a place where we are alone but not lonely. It is the inner quiet place where we come home to our self in God and where we are all ultimately one in the Body of Christ. Solitude is the door to our "inner room" where we may "pray to our Father in secret."

Silence invites us to enter our solitude. Just as there are progressive degrees, dimensions, and depths of silence, so there are increasing levels, dimensions and depths of solitude. Inner silence and solitude bring us to our self, just as we are. They allow us to discover both the poverty and the wealth within us. The sacred space of inner silence and solitude is the place of undressing, where we become naked, intimate and vulnerable before God, who already knows all our secrets and loves us utterly just as we are.

In the sacred space of silence and solitude, as we humbly consent to God's presence and action within us, we may be shown two kinds of truth. One of these concerns our inner poverty and the secrets we have been hiding from our self. This is an essential part of the inner purification and healing process called "unloading the unconscious." The other kind of truth we may be shown reveals aspects of the divine presence within us, such as deep peace, contentment, wellbeing, beauty, joy, and a real sense of being loved by God. A silent breath of preciousness may wash over us or well up inside us.

Whatever happens or does not happen, we accept it *all* as God's grace and will for us in the present moment. God can do only good to us, whether we experience purification or consolation, dry desert or springing fountain. In this we trust because we know by faith that God loves us and all that happens or does not happen in the sacred time and space of our silence, prayer and solitude serves to bring us closer to the divine intimacy and union we seek.

NOTES

1. OUR COMMON GROUND

1. I explore this most important question in my book, *The Will of Divine Love: Centering Prayer and Spiritual Psychology.*

2. See Thomas Keating's *Invitation to Love; Intimacy with God; The Mystery of Christ*; and *The Human Condition.* Also see my *Human Ground Spiritual Ground—Paradise Lost and Found: a Reflection on Centering Prayer's Conceptual Background.*

3. For more about intimacy/belonging in close personal relationships and in relation to society and God see *Human Ground Spiritual Ground*, especially chapters 7, 10, 11, and 12.

4. Thomas Merton gives a clear description of the true and false self in his recorded audio talk, "The True and False Self," recorded live at Gethsemane Monastery; and in *New Seeds of Contemplation*, chapter 38, "Pure Love," pp. 275–289. Also, see the chapters on the false self and the true self in James Finley's valuable book, *Merton's Palace of Nowhere: a Search for God through Awareness of the True Self.*

2. BRIDGING THE THEOLOGICAL DIVIDE

1. This approach has been called "The Hegelian Dialectic," after the German philosopher, Friedrich Hegel (1770–1831).

2. Fr. Bill Sheehan spoke these key words at a conference on "The Soul's Hunger for Intimacy" in Dallas, Texas in March, 2016.

3. Spiritual Journey audio/video series: #2. "Four Levels of Scriptural Experience."

4. I write about the Four Senses of Scripture in *The One Who Loves Us*, chapter 6.

3. FAR AWAY SO CLOSE: THE DIVINE RELATIONSHIP

1. "Far Away So Close" is the title of a 1993 German-language film about the relations between human beings and invisible angels trying to assist them on Earth.

2. *Fruits and Gifts of the Spirit*, pp. 107–108.

3. For more about contemplative attitudes and their cultivation, see David Frenette's wonderful book, *The Path of Centering Prayer: Deepening Your Experience of God.*

4. *The Heart of the World*, p. 40.

5. The term *divine therapy* comes from Thomas Keating—e.g., see *Intimacy with God.*

6. I've written about this in detail in *Human Ground Spiritual Ground: Paradise Lost and Found—a Reflection on Centering Prayer's Conceptual Background.*

7. See *The Return on the Prodigal Son* by Henri Nouwen for an excellent reflection on this parable.

8. The Fruits of the Spirit are: love, joy, peace, patience, kindness, goodness, faithfulness, humility, and self-control. The Gifts of the Spirit are: reverence, fortitude, piety, council, knowledge, understanding, and wisdom. See *Fruits and Gifts of the Spirit* by Thomas Keating for an enlightening treatment of this important topic in Christian Spirituality.

4. THE GIFT OF CONTEMPLATION AND CENTERING PRAYER

1. See/hear Fr. William Meninger's video series on "The Cloud of Unknowing," Set V of "The Christian Contemplative Heritage," produced by Contemplative Outreach (1994).

2. See my book, *The One Who Loves Us*, for a fuller discussion of "rest" and the gift of contemplation in the Judeo–Christian Tradition, pp. 72–74. Gregory the Great (6th century) defined "contemplation" as "resting in God" and "the knowledge of God impregnated with Divine Love."

3. See *Ibid*, chapter 3, "Through a Mystical Christian Window," for more on our inner participation in Jesus' Paschal Mystery and the path of discipleship.

4. "The unconscious" is a vast and mysterious domain of living energies, impulses, and images in the depths of the soul. We may speak of "the unconscious" as a noun, verb, or adjective.

5. See, for example, *Light from Light: an Anthology of Christian Mysticism*, Louis Dupre & James Wiseman, editors; *The Big Book of Christian Mysticism: the Essential Guide to Contemplative Spirituality*, by Carl Mc Colman; *A Taste of Silence* by Carl Arico; and Thomas Keating's audio/video "Spiritual Journey" Series.

6. For more about *Lectio Divina*, see Contemplative Outreach's two Lectio Divina brochures; Maria Tasto's *The Transforming Power of Lectio Divina*; Thomas Keating's *Open Mind, Open Heart*; *A Taste of Silence* by Carl Arico; The Contemplative Life Program praxis on *Lectio Divina* (available from Contemplative Outreach); and my *The One Who Loves Us*, chapter 6.

7. See "Appendix A: The Communion of Mystics" in Carl McColman's *Big Book of Christian Mysticism* (pp. 256–269) for an extensive list of Christian contemplative mystics throughout the ages.

8. See *The Asian Journal of Thomas Merton*, especially pp. 332–333, Appendix IV "Monastic Experience and East–West Dialogue," and Appendix VI "November Circular Letter to Friends."

9. For example, the public dialogues between Cistercians (Trappists) and Buddhists held at Naropa Institute in Boulder, Colorado, 1981–1985, and recorded in *Speaking of Silence: Christians and Buddhists on the Contemplative Way*; and the more private "Snowmass Conferences," organized by Thomas Keating and recorded in *The Common Heart: an Experience of Interreligious Dialogue*.

5. THE METHOD AND PROCESS OF CENTERING PRAYER

1. Though Thomas Merton's untimely death in 1968 was prior to the development of the actual Centering Prayer Method, his prolific writing, teaching, and living example were major inspirations for it. It was Fr. Merton who coined the terms *false self* and *true self*, and it was Merton's speaking of "going to the soul's deepest center in silent contemplation and passing through that center into God" that inspired the name "Centering Prayer."

2. This information and some of what follows comes from a video, "Introduction: the Origins and Inspirations of Centering Prayer," featuring Frs. Thomas Keating, William Meninger, and Basil Pennington. This conference began a 1994 Institute at the Benedictine Center in Beech Grove, Indiana organized by Contemplative Outreach: "The Christian Contemplative Heritage: Our Apophatic Tradition."

3. These and other quotes are from Contemplative Outreach's brochure, "The Method of Centering Prayer."

4. Thomas Keating's books, *Open Mind, Open Heart* and *Intimacy with God*; Carl Arico's *A Taste of Silence* and his video "Centering Prayer, A Way of Life," on the Four Guidelines; David Muyskens' *Forty Days to a Closer Walk with God*; Murchadh O'Madagain's *Centering Prayer and the Healing of the Unconscious*; David Frenette's *The Path of Centering Prayer*; and Peter Traben Haas' *A Beautiful Prayer, Answering Common Misperceptions About Centering Prayer* are all very helpful for understanding the Method of Centering Prayer and its Christian context.

5. For an enlightening discussion of the Christian Mystical Tradition in the context of *apophatic* prayer, see Thomas Merton's book, *Contemplative Prayer*. This book describes both the prayer and its process of inner transformation from the perspective of a dedicated and well-educated Cistercian Monk.

6. "Introduction: Origins and Inspirations of Centering Prayer" video.

7. For more about this, see chapter 3 of my book, *The Will of Divine Love*, "God's Great Adventure, part three, Tielhard de Chardin's Curve of Evolution." Also see Fr. De Chardin's books: *Man's Place in Nature*; *The Future of Man*; and *Christianity and Evolution: Reflections on Science and Religion*.

8. I discuss the Paschal Mystery as a model of the soul's inner transformation in Christ in chapter 2 of my book *The One Who Loves Us*, "Through a Mystical Christian Window." Also see *The Mystery of Christ* by Thomas Keating.

9. In the early 1990s, the "Eternal Word Television Network" (EWTN) launched an alarming thirteen-part series: "The New Age, Satan's Counterfeit." Part Three of this series, "Meditation and Centering Prayer," presents an ill-informed and inaccurate attack against the method of Centering Prayer.

10. I discuss the topic of outer and inner spiritual influences in my book, *The Will of Divine Love*. See chapter 4, "Good versus Evil: the Archetypal Conflict," and chapter 5, "Centering Prayer and Spiritual Psychology."

11. *Ibid.* chapter 6: "Centering Prayer and Jungian Psychology."

6. Affirming and Negating Centering Prayer

1. See/hear *Heartfulness: Transformation in Christ*, the book and audio/DVD set that features Thomas Keating being interviewed by Betty Sue Flowers, available from Contemplative Outreach.

2. *The Better Part* by Thomas Keating offers a profound and instructive reflection on the "Martha and Mary" story.

3. See Thomas Keating's *The Mystery of Christ* and my *The One Who Loves Us*, chapter 3.

4. We'd been viewing Thomas Keating's "Spiritual Journey" video series, studying *Open Mind, Open Heart*; *Invitation to Love*; *The Mystery of Christ*; *The Cloud of Unknowing*; and other helpful books.

5. These anti-Centering Prayer critics included: Mother M. Angelica, who founded EWTN and wrote that Centering Prayer is "a form of eastern mysticism, that is both misleading and dangerous to the faithful;" Johnette Benkovic and Fr. Emile Lafranz who agree that Centering Prayer is "Transcendental Meditation in a Christian Dress;" a Ms. Sue Thompson, who gives anti-Centering Prayer testimony that's reproduced in a dossier I received; and Fr. Finbarr Flanagan, who also equates Centering Prayer to TM.

6. The Charismatic Ministry leader's name is Johnette Benkovic.

7. For example, there are numerous positive personal testimonials to the human, social, and spiritual benefits of Centering Prayer posted on the website www.contemplativeoutreach.org under "Voices of Grace and Gratitude."

8. *The Documents of Vatican II*, p. 470: "*... as they seek God before all things and only Him, the members of each* [religious] *community should combine contemplation with apostolic love. By the former they adhere to God in mind and heart; by the latter they strive to associate themselves with the work of redemption and to spread the Kingdom of God.*"

9. The people involved in EWTN's "Satan's Counterfeit" were active Charismatic Catholic Christians. See Notes 5 and 6 above

10. "Anthem" on disc 2 of *The Essential Leonard Cohen*.

7. CALMING THE TROUBLED WATERS

1. In *Fruits and Gifts of the Spirit*, Thomas Keating gives a fine and detailed explanation of these gifts.

2. Two of these relatively recent critics are 1) Connie Rossini, author of: *Is Centering Prayer Catholic? Thomas Keating Meets Teresa of Avila and the CDF* (2015); and whose articles have appeared in EWTN's online News and elsewhere. 2) Sharon Lee Giganti, who is a frequent guest on EWTN radio's "Catholic Answers" and whose website www.newagedeception.com has, under the "Free Resources" tab, "Seven Reasons Why the Errors in the Centering Prayer Movement Should Not Be in Your Parish," (2009).

3. This article may be found in *The Thomas Keating Reader* and in the Contemplative Outreach Newsletter, Volume 7, Number 1—Spring 1993 (available on the CO Website).

4. Ibid, pp. 43–44.

5. *Pocket Dictionary of Theological Terms*, p. 80.

6. See note 2 this chapter.

7. *Meditations on the Parables of Jesus*, pp. 121–126.

8. In *The One Who Loves Us: Centering Prayer and Evolving* Consciousness, I discuss differing "Christian Windows" wherein our beloved conservative traditionalist fellow Christians belong to the "traditional stage of evolving consciousness," as do the most of the world's major organized religions.

9. *Ibid*. The "Christian Windows" correlate to the "tribal," "warrior," "traditional," "modern," "postmodern," and "integral" stages of evolving consciousness as identified in Ken Wilber's Integral Theory.

10. *Is Centering Prayer Catholic?* See p. 56 and the very brief chapters regarding Prayer, Contemplation, and *Lectio Divina*.

11. In Teresa's *Interior Castle*—which moves through the "First Dwelling Places" at the soul's periphery to the "Seventh Dwelling Places" in its true center (the place of "full union")—the stages of prayer include "reading of Scripture" and "the practice of virtue," "vocal prayer," "mental prayer," "affective prayer," "the prayer of simplicity" or "active recollection" (which corresponds to Centering Prayer). These are the types of prayer that we may initiate and carryout in relating to God. Beyond "the prayer

of simplicity" (active recollection of the faculties), we become receptive as the divine action takes the initiative, bringing us through the deeper stages of the gift of infused *apophatic* contemplation (represented by the Fourth through Seventh Mansions or Dwelling Places); that is, "infused recollection," "prayer of quiet," "prayer of union," and "prayer of full union." Teresa describes all of these in detail in *The Interior Castle*.

8. DIVIDES AND THEIR CROSSING

1. The basics of God's Creation process (according to the ancient Qabalah) are detailed in *Centering Prayer and Rebirth in Christ on the Tree of Life*, pp. 12–20.

2. See Note 7, chapter 5.

3. See *The Will of Divine Love*, chapter 4, for details regarding this divide in human nature.

9. BRIDGING CREATED REALITY TO NON-CREATED REALITY

1. *The Mystery of Christ*, p. 60.

2. I first wrote of these "Three Types of Consciousness" in *The Creation of Reality* (1986), pp. 144–150.

3. This process is detailed in my book, *Centering Prayer and Rebirth in Christ on the Tree of Life*.

4. Lorenna McKinnett's rendering, from her CDs, "The Mask and the Mirror," and "The Journey So Far," (deluxe two-CD edition).

5. See Note 11, chapter 7 above.

Suggestions for Further Study

In addition to the written and recorded works of Thomas Keating, I suggest the following for enriching our appreciation of Centering Prayer and its place as an important contemporary expression of the Christian Contemplative Tradition:

Books:

Fr. Carl J. Arico: *A Taste of Silence: A Guide to the Fundamentals of Centering Prayer.*

Rev. Dr. Cynthia Bourgeault: *The Heart of Centering Prayer: Christian Nonduality in Theory and Practice.*

David Frenette: *The Path of Centering Prayer: Deepening Your Experience of God.*

Fr. Thomas Merton: *Contemplative Prayer*; and *The Inner Experience.*

Rev. David Myskens: *Forty Days to a Closer Walk with God: The Practice of Centering Prayer.*

Fr. Murchadh Ó Madagáin: *Centering Prayer and the Healing of the Unconscious.*

Rev. Dr. Peter Traben Haas: *A Beautiful Prayer: Answering Common Misperceptions about Centering Prayer.*

Online:

Rev. David Myskens: "Protestant Barriers to Contemplative Prayer." www.contemplaticeoutreach.org; 2011 Contemplative Outreach News and October 2016, CO e-bulletin.

Deborah Ann Foster: "The Church in the Wilderness: Christianity's Conflict with Contemplative Prayer." Master's Thesis, Vancouver School of Theology. Available at: https://open.library.ubc.ca/cIRcle/collection/graduateresearch/46280/items/1.0103032.

REFERENCES

Anonymous. *The Cloud of Unknowing* (ed. W. Johnston). New York: Doubleday, 1973.

Arico, C. *A Taste of Silence*. New York: Lantern, 2015.

Bourgeault, C. *The Heart of Centering Prayer: Nondual Christianity in Theory and Practice*. Boulder, CO: Shambhala, 2016.

Cassian, J. *Conferences* (C. Luibheid, tr.) *Classics of Western Spirituality*. New York: Paulist Press, 1985.

Catechism of the Catholic Church, 2nd ed. Washington, DC: Liberia Editrice Vaticana, 1997.

Contemplative Life Program. *Lectio Divina*. Butler, NJ: Contemplative Outreach, 2005.

de Chardin. P. T. *Christianity and Evolution*. New York: Harcourt, 1971.

———. *The Future of Man*. New York: Doubleday, 1964.

———. *Man's Place in Nature*. New York: Harper, 1966.

DOSSIER (privately circulated) T. Keating, G. Fitzpatrick-Hopler, *et al*. Butler, NJ: Contemplative Outreach, 1992.

Dupré, L. and J. Wiseman (eds.). *Light From Light: An Anthology of Christian Mysticism*. New York: Paulist Press, 1988.

Finley, J. *Merton's Palace of Nowhere*. Notre Dame, IN: Ave Maria Press, 1978.

Frenette, D. *The Path of Centering Prayer: Deepening Your Experience of God*. Boulder, CO: Sounds True, 2012.

Frey, K. *Centering Prayer and Rebirth in Christ on the Tree of Life: The Process of Inner Transformation*. Great Barrington, MA: Portal Books, 2013.

———. *The Creation of Reality*. Marina del Rey, CA: De Vorss, 1986.

———. *Human Ground Spiritual Ground: Paradise Lost and Found*. Great Barrington, MA: Portal Books, 2012.

———. *The One Who Loves Us: Centering Prayer and Evolving Consciousness*. Great Barrington, MA: Portal Books, 2014.

———. *The Will of Divine Love: Centering Prayer and Spiritual Psychology*. Great Barrington, MA: Lindisfarne Books, 2016.

Grenz, S. J., C. Guretzki, and C. F. Norling. *Pocket Dictionary of Theological Terms*. Downers Grove, IL: InterVarsity Press, 1999.

Hauser, R. *In His Spirit: A Guide to Today's Spirituality*. New York: Paulist Press, 1982.

Holy Bible: King James Version. London: Collins Clear-Type Press, 1957.

Holy Bible: New Revised Standard Version. New York: Oxford Univ. Press, 1989.

John of the Cross, Saint. *The Collected Works of St. John of the Cross* (tr. K. Kavanaugh and O. Rodriguez). Washington, DC: ECS, 1978.

Keating, T. *The Better Part.* New York: Continuum, 2000.

———. *Fruits and Gifts of the Spirit.* New York: Lantern, 2000.

———. *The Heart of the World.* New York: Crossroad, 1988.

———. *The Human Condition: Contemplation and Transformation.* New York: Paulist, 1999.

———. *Intimacy with God: An Introduction to Centering Prayer.* New York: Crossroad, 2009.

———. *Invitation to Love: The Way of Christian Contemplation.* New York: Continuum, 1992.

———. *Meditations on the Parables of Jesus.* New York: Crossroad, 2010.

———. *The Mystery of Christ: The Liturgy as Spiritual Experience.* New York: Continuum, 2003.

———. *Open Mind, Open Heart: The Contemplative Dimension of the Gospel.* New York: Continuum, 2006.

———. *The Thomas Keating Reader: Selected Writings from the Contemplative Outreach Newsletter.* New York: Lantern, 2012.

McColman, C. *The Big Book of Christian Mysticism: The Essential Guide to Contemplative Spirituality.* Charlottesville, VA: Hampton Roads, 2010.

Meninger, W. *The Loving Search for God: Contemplative Prayer and the Cloud of Unknowing.* New York: Continuum, 1994.

St. John of the Cross for Beginners. New York: Lantern, 2014.

Merton, T. *The Asian Journal of Thomas Merton.* New York: New Directions, 1973.

———. *Contemplative Prayer.* New York: Doubleday, 1990

———. *The Inner Experience: Notes on Contemplation* (W. Shannon, ed.). San Francisco: Harper, 2003.

———. *New Seeds of Contemplation.* New York: New Directions, 1961.

Miles-Yépez, N., ed. *The Common Heart: An Experience of Interreligious Dialogue.* New York: Lantern Books, 2006.

Myskens, D. *Forty Days to a Closer Walk with God: The Practice of Centering Prayer.* Nashville, TN: Upper Room, 2006.

The New American Bible. New York: Catholic Book Publishing, 1986.

Nouwen, H. *The Return of the Prodigal Son: A Story of Homecoming.* New York: Doubleday, 1992.

Ó Madagáin, M. *Centering Prayer and the Healing of the Unconscious.* New York: Lantern, 2007.

Papal Documents: *Letter to the Bishops of the Catholic Church on Some Aspects of Christian Meditation* (Vatican trans.). Congregation for the Doctrine of the Faith, Boston: St. Paul Books.

———. *The Documents of Vatican II* (Rev. J. Gallagher, tr. & ed.). New York: Guild Press, 1966.

———. "Jesus Christ the Bearer of the Water of Life." Pontifical Councils for Culture and Religious Dialogue.

Rossini, C. *Is Centering Prayer Catholic? Fr. Thomas Keating Meets Teresa of Avila and the CDF.* New Ulm, MN: Four Waters Press, 2015.

Tasto, M. *The Transforming Power of Lectio Divina: How to Pray with Scripture.* New London, CT: Twenty-Third Publications, 2013.

Teresa of Avila, Saint. *The Interior Castle* (tr., K. Kavanaugh and O. Rodroguez) *Classics of Western Spirituality.* Mahwah, NJ: Paulist Press, 1979.

Traben Haas, P. *A Beautiful Prayer: Answering Common Misperceptions about Centering Prayer.* Austin, TX: Contemplative Christians, 2014.

Walker, S., editor. *Speaking of Silence.* New York: Paulist Press, 1987.

OTHER REFERENCES

Audio:

Leonard Cohen: "Anthem." *The Essential Leonard Cohen,* disc 2. Columbia/Sony Music, 2002.

Loreena McKinnett: *The Mask and the Mirror.* Quinlan Rd., 1994.

Thomas Merton: *The True and False Self.* Kansas City, MO: National Catholic Reporter, 1988.

Video:

Thomas Keating: The Spiritual Journey Series; and *Heartfulness: Transformation in Christ,* with Betty Sue Flowers. Contemplative Outreach online store.

Fr. Carl J. Arico: *Centering Prayer: A Way of Life.* Contemplative Outreach, 2016.

Frs. Thomas Keating, William Meninger and Basil Pennington: *The Christian Contemplative Heritage: Our Apophatic Tradition:* "Introduction: the Origins and Inspirations of Centering Prayer"; and *The Cloud of Unknowing,* with William Meninger. Contemplative Outreach, 1994.

Far Away, So Close! Germany, Wim Wenders, Director (English subtitles): CFP Video, 1993.

CONTEMPLATIVE OUTREACH is a spiritual network of individuals and small faith communities committed to living the contemplative dimension of the Gospel. The common desire for Divine transformation, primarily expressed through a commitment to a daily Centering Prayer practice, unites our international, interdenominational community.

Today, Contemplative Outreach annually serves over 40,000 people; supports more than 120 active contemplative chapters in 39 countries; supports more than 800 prayer groups; teaches more than 15,000 people the practice of Centering Prayer and other contemplative practices through locally hosted workshops; and provides training and resources to local chapters and volunteers. We also publish and distribute the wisdom teachings of Fr. Thomas Keating and other resources that support the contemplative life.

Contemplative Outreach, Ltd.
10 Park Place, 2nd Floor, Suite B
Butler, New Jersey 07405

973-838-3384
Fax 973-492-5795
Email: office@coutreach.org
www.contemplativeoutreach.org

KESS FREY was born in 1945 and grew up in the Eagle Rock neighborhood of North Los Angeles. In 1968, he graduated in Psychology at the University of California, Irvine. He has studied Eastern and Western philosophy, psychology, and religion since 1965, with particular interests in meditation and depth psychology. He was raised Catholic and is a Catholic Christian who honors the contemplative dimension of all religions and spiritual paths. His principal spiritual teachers have been Lama Anagarika Govinda (German), Chogyam Trungpa, Rinpoche (Tibetan), Swami Amar Jyoti (East Indian), and, since 1989, Fr. Thomas Keating (American).

Mr. Frey has lived in Anchorage, Alaska since 1983, where he worked with school-age children for twenty years. He has been involved with Centering Prayer since 1989, is affiliated with Contemplative Outreach, Ltd., and offers introductory Centering Prayer workshops, facilitates prayer groups and silent retreats, and is active in prison ministry. He is the author of six previous books: *Satsang Notes of Swami Amar Jyoti* (1977); *The Creation of Reality* (1986); *Human Ground, Spiritual Ground: Paradise Lost and Found: A Reflection on Centering Prayer's Conceptual Background* (2012); *Centering Prayer and Rebirth in Christ on the Tree of Life: The Process of Inner Transformation* (2013); *The One Who Loves Us: Centering Prayer and Evolving Consciousness* (2014) and most recently, *The Will of Divine Love: Centering Prayer and Spiritual Psychology* (2016).

CPSIA information can be obtained
at www.ICGtesting.com
Printed in the USA
LVOW12s0848040617
536873LV00001B/85/P